The Richest Man in Babylon

Now Revised and Updated for the 21st Century

George S. Clason

10/2008 GenFun $20

© Copyright 2007 – BN Publishing

www.bnpublishing.com

info@bnpublishing.com

Printed in the U.S.A.

CONTENTS

THE TALE OF THE MAN WHO DESIRED MUCH GOLD

BANSIR, the chariot builder of Babylon, was thoroughly discouraged. From his seat upon the low wall surrounding his property, he gazed sadly at his simple home and the open workshop in which stood a partially completed chariot.

His wife frequently appeared at the open door. Her furtive glances in his direction reminded him that the meal bag was almost empty and he should be at work finishing the chariot, hammering and hewing, polishing and painting, stretching taut the leather over the wheel rims, preparing it for delivery so he could collect from his wealthy customer.

Nevertheless, his fat, muscular body sat stolidly upon the wall. His slow mind was struggling patiently with a problem for which he could find no answer. The hot, tropical sun, so typical of this valley of the Euphrates, beat down upon him mercilessly. Beads of perspiration formed upon his brow and trickled down unnoticed to lose themselves in the hairy jungle on his chest.

Beyond his home towered the high terraced walls surrounding the king's palace. Nearby, cleaving the blue heavens, was the painted tower to the Temple of Bel. In the shadow of such grandeur was his simple home and many others far less neat and well cared for. Babylon was like this - a mixture of grandeur and squalor, of dazzling wealth and direst poverty, crowded together without plan or system within the protecting walls of the city.

Behind him, had he cared to turn and look, the noisy chariots of the rich, jostled and crowded aside the sandaled tradesmen as well as the barefooted beggars. Even the rich, in turn, were forced to turn into the gutters to clear the way for the long lines of slave water carriers, on the "King's Business", each bearing a heavy goat skin of water to be poured upon the hanging gardens.

Bansir was too engrossed in his own problem to hear or heed the confused hubbub of the busy city. It was the unexpected twanging of the strings from a familiar lyre that aroused him from his reverie. He turned and looked into the sensitive, smiling face of his best friend - Kobbi, the musician.

"May God bless you with great liberality, my good friend", began Kobbi with an elaborate salute. "Yet, it appears he has already been so generous that you need not labor. I rejoice with you in your good fortune. Moreover, I would even share it with you. Kindly extract but two humble shekels from your purse which must be bulging – or else you would be working busily in your shop – and lend them to me until after the noblemen's feast tonight. You will not even miss them before they are returned."

"If I did have two shekels", Bansir responded gloomily, "I could lend them to no one – not even to you, my best friend; for they would be my fortune - my entire fortune. No one lends his entire fortune, not even to his best friend."

"What!" exclaimed Kobbi with genuine surprise, 'You haven't a single shekel in your purse, yet you sit like a statue upon a wall! Why not finish that chariot? How else can you feed yourself? This is not like you, my friend. Where is your endless energy? Is something distressing you?

"It must be a torment from God," Bansir agreed. "It began with a dream, a senseless dream, in which I thought I was a man of means. From my belt hung a handsome purse, heavy with coins. There were shekels which I cast with careless freedom to the beggars; there were pieces of silver with which I bought finery for my wife and whatever I desired for myself; there were pieces of gold which made me feel assured of the future and unafraid to spend the silver. I had a glorious feeling of contentment! You wouldn't have recognized me as your hard-working friend. Nor would you have known my wife, so free from wrinkles was her face and shining with happiness. She was again the smiling maiden of our early married days."

8

"A pleasant dream, indeed," commented Kobbi, "but why should such pleasant feelings turn you into a glum statue upon the wall?"

"Why, indeed! Because when I awoke and remembered how empty my purse was, a rebellious feeling came over me. Let's talk it over, for, as the sailors say, we ride in the same boat, the two of us. As youngsters, we learned wisdom together from the priests. As young men, we shared each other's pleasures. As grown men, we have always been close friends. We have been contented subjects of our king. We have been satisfied to work long hours and spend our earnings freely. We have earned many coins in the years that have passed, yet we can but dream of the joys that come from wealth. Bah! Are we not more than dumb sheep? We live in the richest city in the whole world. Travelers say none equals it in wealth. All around us are displays of wealth, but we possess none of it ourselves. After half a lifetime of hard labor, you, my best of friends, have an empty purse and ask me, 'May I borrow a mere two shekels until after the noblemen's feast tonight'? Then, what do I reply? Do I say here is my purse; its contents I will gladly share? No, I admit that my purse is as empty as yours. *What is the matter? Why can't we acquire silver and gold beyond the bare necessities of life?*

"Consider, also, our sons," Bansir continued, "are they not following in the footsteps of their fathers? Need they and their families and their sons and their sons' families live all their lives in the midst of such treasures of gold, and yet, like us, be content to eat sour milk and porridge?"

"Never, in all the years of our friendship, have I heard you speak like this before, Bansir." Kobbi was puzzled.

"Never in all these years did I think like this before. From early dawn until darkness, I have labored to build the finest chariots any man could make, soft heartedly hoping that some day God would recognize my worthy deeds and grant me great prosperity. This he has never done. At last, I realize this he will never do. Therefore, my heart is sad. I want to be a man of means. I want to own lands and cattle, to have fine clothing and money in my purse. I am willing to work for these things with all my strength, with all the skill in my hands, with all the cunning in my mind, but I want my labors to be fairly rewarded. What's the matter with us? Again I ask you! Why can't we have our just share of the good things, or the gold with which to buy them?"

"I wish I had an answer!" Kobbi replied. "I am no more satisfied than you. My earnings from my lyre are quickly gone. Often I have to plan and scheme so that my family won't be hungry. I have also yearned for a lyre large enough that could truly sing the strains of music surging through my mind. With such an instrument I could make music finer than even the king has heard before."

"Such a lyre you ought to have. No man in all of Babylon could make it sing more sweetly; so sweetly that not only the king but God himself would be delighted. But how can you attain it while we both of us are as poor as the king's slaves?. Listen to the bell! Here they come." He pointed to the long column of half naked, sweating water bearers plodding laboriously up the narrow street from the river. Five abreast they marched, each bent under a heavy goatskin of water.

"A strong-figured man, their leader is", Kobbi indicated the bell wearer who marched in front without a load.

"There are many fine men in the line," Bansir agreed, "as good as we are. Tall, blond men from the north, laughing black men from the south, little brown men from the nearer countries. All marching together from the river to the gardens, back and forth, day after day, year after year. Yet, they have not an ounce of happiness to look forward to – only beds of straw upon which to sleep and hard porridge to eat. Pity the poor brutes, Kobbi!"

"Pity them I do. Yet, you make me realize how little better off we are, though we call ourselves free men."

'That is the truth, Kobbi, unpleasant though it may be. We've had enough of living slavish lives, year after year. Working, working, working! Getting nowhere."

"Could we not find out how others acquire gold and do as they do?" Kobbi inquired.

"Perhaps there is some secret we might learn if we searched out those who know", replied Bansir thoughtfully.

"'Just today," suggested Kobbi, "I passed our old friend, Arkad, riding in his golden chariot. He didn't look over my head and ignore me as many in his station might consider his right. Instead, he waved at me for all to see as he bestowed his smile of friendship on his friend Kobbi, the musician."

"'He is claimed to be the richest man in all of Babylon," Bansir mused.

"So rich, the king is said to seek his golden aid in affairs of the treasury. Arkad has an income that constantly keeps his purse full, no matter how freely he spends." Kobbi replied.

"Income, that's it!" exclaimed Bansir. "I want an income that will keep flowing into my purse whether I sit upon the wall or travel to far lands. Arkad must know how a man can make an income for himself. Do you suppose he could teach a mind as slow as mine?"

"I don't see why not; he taught his knowledge to his son, Nomasir," Kobbi responded. "Wasn't he the one who went to Nineveh and became, without aid from his father, one of the richest men in that city?"

"Kobbi, you are giving me a great idea." A new light gleamed in Bansir's eyes. "It costs nothing to ask wise advice from a good friend, and Arkad was always that. Never mind that our purses are empty – let that not detain us. We are tired of being without gold in the midst of plenty. We want to become men of means. Come, let's go to Arkad and ask how we, also, can earn an income for ourselves."

'You speak wisely, Bansir, and help me begin to understand why we have never found any measure of wealth. We never sought it. You labored patiently to build the staunchest chariots in Babylon and devoted yourself wholeheartedly to that purpose. Therefore, you succeeded at it. I strove to become a skilful lyre player, and at that, I, too succeeded."

"For those things in which we exerted our best efforts, we succeeded. Now, at last, we see the light: it beckons us to learn more so that we may prosper more. This is the wisest thing we have ever done. *With a new understanding we can find honorable ways to fulfill our desires."*

"Let's go to Arkad today," Bansir urged. "Also, let's ask our other friends, who have fared no better than us, to join us so that they, too, may share in his wisdom".

"You were always thoughtful of your friends, Bansir. Therefore, you have many. We will do as you say. We'll go to Arkad today and take our friends with us."

THE RICHEST MAN IN BABYLON TELLS HIS SYSTEM

IN Old Babylon there once lived a certain very rich man named Arkad. Far and wide he was famed for his great wealth. He was also famed for his liberality. He was generous in his charities. He was generous with his family. He was liberal in his own expenses. But nevertheless, each year his wealth increased more rapidly than he spent it.

And there were certain friends of younger days who came to him and said: "You, Arkad, are more fortunate than we. You have become the richest man in all of Babylon while we struggle for existence. You wear the finest garments and you enjoy rare foods, while we must be content to clothe our families in attire barely presentable and feed them as best we can.

"Yet, once we were equal. We studied under the same master; we played the same games, and in neither did you outshine us. And in the years since, you have been no more an honorable citizen than we have.

"Nor have you worked harder or more faithfully, in so far as we can judge. Why, then, should a fickle fate single you out to enjoy all the good things of life and ignore us who are equally deserving?"

Thereupon Arkad replied, "If you have not acquired more than a bare existence in the years since we were youths, it is because you have either have failed to learn the laws that govern the building of wealth, or else you did not observe them.

"'Fickle fate' is a notion that doesn't bring permanent good to anyone. On the contrary, those who acquire unearned gold soon spend all they receive, and are left with overwhelming appetites and desires they have not the ability to gratify. Yet others become misers and hoard their wealth, afraid to spend what they have, knowing they do not possess the ability to replace it. They are further beset by fear of robbers and doom themselves to lives of emptiness and secret misery.

"There are probably others, who can take unearned gold and add to it and continue to be happy and contented citizens. But they are so few in number, I know of them only by hearsay. Think of the men you know who have inherited sudden wealth, and see if what I say is not so."

His friends admitted that of the men they knew who had inherited wealth these words were true, and they begged him to explain to them how he had attained so much property, so he continued:

"In my youth, I looked around and saw all the good things that could bring happiness and contentment. And I realized that wealth increased the potency of all these.

"Wealth is a power. With wealth many things are possible.

"One may ornament one's home with the richest of furnishings.

"One may sail the distant seas.

"One may feast on delicacies of far lands.

"One may buy gold and precious stones.

"One may even build mighty temples for God.

"One may do all these things and many others which delight the senses and gratify the soul.

"And when I realized all this, I declared to myself that I would claim my share of the good things of life. I would not be one of those who stand by, enviously watching others enjoy. I would not be content to clothe myself in the cheapest attire that looked respectable. I would not be satisfied with the lot of a poor man. On the contrary, I would make myself a guest at this banquet of good things.

"Being, as you know, the son of a humble merchant, one of a large family with no hope of an inheritance, and not being endowed – as you have so frankly pointed out – with superior powers or wisdom, I decided that if I was to achieve what I desired, time and study would be required.

"As for time, all men have it in abundance. You, each of you, have let sufficient time slip by to have had made yourselves wealthy. Yet, you admit you have nothing to show except your good families, of which you can be justly proud.

"As for study, didn't our wise teacher teach us that learning was of two kinds: one kind being the things we learned and knew, and the other being in the training that taught us how to find out what we did not know?

"Therefore, I decided to find out how one might accumulate wealth, and when I had found out, to make this my task and do it well.

"I found employment as a scribe in the hall of records, and labored long hours each day upon the clay tablets. Week after week, and month after month, I labored, yet I had nothing to show for my earnings – food, clothing and penance to God absorbed all my earnings. But my determination did not leave me.

"And one day Algamish, the money lender, came to my place of employment and ordered a copy of the Ninth Law, and he said to me, 'I must have this in two days, and if the task is done by that time, I will give you two coppers.'

"I labored hard, but the law was long, and when Algamish returned the task was unfinished. He was angry, but knowing my master would not permit him to injure me, I was unafraid, so I said to him:

"'Algamish, you are a very rich man. Tell me how I, too, may become rich, and I will labor all night to complete your carving.

15

"He smiled at me and replied, 'You are a brazen lad, but we will call it a bargain.'

"All that night I carved, though my back hurt and the smell of the wick made my head ache until my eyes could hardly see. But when he returned at sun-up the tablets were complete.

"'Now,' I said, 'tell me what you promised.''

"'You have fulfilled your part of our bargain, my son,' he said to me kindly, 'and I am ready to fulfill mine. I will tell you these things you wish to know because I am getting old, and an old tongue loves to wag. And when youth comes to age for advice he receives the wisdom of years. Too often, youth thinks the aged know only the wisdom of days gone by. But remember this: the sun that shines today is the sun that shone when your father was born, and will still be shining when your last grandchild passes on.

"The thoughts of youth," he continued, "are bright things that shine forth like the meteors that often light up the sky, but the wisdom of old age is like the fixed stars that shine so steadfastly that sailors depend upon them to steer their course.

"Mark you well my words, for if you don't, you will fail to grasp the truth that I will tell you, and you will think that your night's work has been in vain."

"Then he looked at me shrewdly from under his shaggy brows and said in a low, forceful tone, 'I found the road to wealth when I decided that *a part of all I earned was mine to keep.* And so will you.'

"Then he continued to look at me with a glance that I could feel pierce me but said no more.

"'Is that all?' I asked.

"That was sufficient to change the heart of a sheep herder into the heart of a money lender,' he replied.

16

"'But *all* I earn is mine to keep, is it not? I demanded.

"'Far from it,' he replied. 'Do you not pay the clothing stores? Do you not pay the shoemakers? Do you not pay for the things you eat? Can you live in Babylon without spending? What do you have left of your earnings to show for the past month? For the past year? Fool! You pay everyone but yourself. You labor for others. You may as well be a slave and work for what your master gives you to eat and wear. However, if you kept for yourself one-tenth of all you earned, how much would you have in ten years?'

"My mathematical skills did not desert me, and I answered, 'As much as I earn in one year.'

"'You speak but half the truth', he retorted. 'Every gold piece you save is like a slave that works for you. Every copper it earns is like its child that can also earn for you. If you wish to become wealthy, then what you save must earn, and its children must earn, and its children's children must earn, so that you may acquire the abundance you crave.

"'You may think I am cheating you for your long night's work,' he continued, 'but I am paying you a thousand times over if you have the intelligence to grasp the truth I offer you.

"'A PART OF ALL YOU EARN IS YOURS TO KEEP. It should not be less than a tenth no matter how little you earn. It can be as much more as you can afford. Pay yourself first. Do not buy from the clothing store and the shoemaker more than you can pay out of the rest and still have enough left over for food and charity and penance to God.

"'Wealth, like a tree, grows from a tiny seed. The first copper you save is the seed from which your tree of wealth will grow. The sooner you plant that seed, the sooner the tree can grow. And the more faithfully you nourish and water that tree with consistent savings, the sooner may you bask in contentment under its shade.' So saying, he took his tablets and went away.

"I thought a great deal about what he had said to me, and it seemed reasonable. So I decided I would try it. Each time I was paid, I took one from each ten pieces of copper and hid it away. And strange as it may seem, I was no shorter of funds than before. I noticed little difference as I managed to get along without it. Often, as my savings grew, I was tempted to spend it on some of the good things the merchants displayed, brought by camels and ships from the land of the Phoenicians. But I wisely refrained.

"A year later, Algamish returned and said to me, 'Son, have you paid yourself not less than one tenth of all you have earned for the past year?'

"I answered proudly, 'Yes, master, I have.'

"That is good,' he answered beaming upon me, 'And what have you done with it?'

"'I gave it to Azmur, the brick maker, who told me he was traveling over the seven seas, and in Tyre he will buy me rare jewels from the Phoenicians. When he returns, we shall sell these at high prices and divide the earnings.'

"'Every fool must learn,' he growled, 'but why trust the knowledge of a brick maker about jewels? Would you go to the bread maker to inquire about the stars? No, you would go to an astrologer, if you had the power to think. Your savings are gone, lad, you have jerked your wealth tree up by the roots. But plant another. Try again. And next time, if you want advice about jewels, go to the jewel merchant. If you want to know about sheep, go to the herdsman. Advice is one thing that is freely given away, but watch that you take only what is worth having. One who takes advice about his savings from one who is inexperienced in such matters, will pay with his savings.' Saying this, he went away.

"And it happened just as he said. For the Phoenicians are scoundrels and they sold Azmur worthless bits of glass that looked like gems. But as Algamish had instructed me, I again saved each tenth copper, and it was no longer difficult for it had now become a habit.

"A year later Algamish again came to the room of the scribes and addressed me. 'What progress have you made since last I saw you?

"'I have paid myself faithfully,' I replied, 'and I entrusted my savings to Agger the shield maker, to buy bronze, and every four months he pays me a rental fee.'

"That is good. And what do you do with the rental money?

"I have a great feast with honey and fine wine and spiced cake. I also bought myself a purple tunic. And some day I will buy myself a young donkey to ride upon.'

"To which Algamish laughed. 'If you eat and spend the children of your savings, then how do you expect them to earn for you? And how can they have children that will also earn for you? First acquire for yourself an army of golden slaves; then you may enjoy many rich banquets without regret.' And so saying, he went away again.

"I did not see him again for two years, when he once more returned, and his face was full of deep lines and his eyes drooped, for he was getting old. And he said to me, "Arkad, have you achieved the wealth you dreamed of yet?

"And I answered, 'Not all that I desire yet, but I have earned some, and what I have earns more, and its earnings earn more.'

"'And do you still take the advice from brick makers?'

"'About brick making, they give good advice,' I retorted.

"Arkad," he continued, 'you have learned your lessons well. You first learned to live on less money that you earned. Next you learned to seek advice from those who were competent through their own experiences to give it. And, lastly, you have learned to make gold work for you.

"'You have taught yourself how to acquire money, how to keep it, and how to use it. Therefore, you are competent for a responsible position. I am getting old, and my sons think only of spending money, with no thought to earning. I have many interests that I can no longer look after. If you will go to Nippur and look after my lands there, I will make you my partner and you will share in my estate.'

"So I went to Nippur and took charge of his holdings, which were large. And because I was full of ambition and because I had mastered the three laws of successfully handling wealth, I was able to greatly increase the value of his properties. So I prospered, and when Algamish passed away, I inherited the shares he left me in his estate."

So spoke Arkad, and when he finished his tale, one of his friends said, "You were indeed fortunate that Algamish made you an heir."

"I was fortunate only in that I had the desire to prosper before I first met him. Did I not prove for four years my definiteness of purpose by keeping one tenth of all I earned? Would you call a fisherman 'lucky' who for years studied the habits of fish so that he could skillfully catch them in his nets? Opportunity is a proud goddess who wastes no time with those who are unprepared."

"You had strong will power to keep going after you lost your first year's savings. You are unusual in that way," spoke up another.

"Will power!" retorted Arkad. "What nonsense. Do you think will power gives a man the strength to lift a burden that a camel cannot carry, or to draw a load that the oxen cannot budge? Will power is but the unwavering intention to carry a task you set for yourself to completion. If I set for myself a task, be it ever so trivial, I will see it through. How else can I have confidence in myself to do important things? If I said to myself, 'For a hundred days, as I walk across the bridge into the city, I will pick up a stone from the road and throw it into the stream,' I would do it. If on the seventh day I passed by without remembering, I wouldn't say to myself, "Tomorrow I'll throw two stones which will do just as well.' Instead, I would retrace my steps and throw in the stone. Nor on the twentieth day would I say to myself, 'Arkad, this is useless. What does it help you to throw a stone every day? Just throw in a handful of stones and be done with it.' No, I would not say nor do that. When I set a task for myself, I complete it. Therefore, I'm careful not to start difficult and impractical tasks, because I love leisure."

And then another friend spoke up and said, "If what you tell is true, and it does seem, as you said – reasonable, then being so simple, if all men did it, there wouldn't be enough wealth to go around."

"Wealth grows wherever men exert energy," Arkad replied. "If a rich man builds himself a new palace, is the gold he pays out gone? No, the brick maker has part of it and the laborer has part of it, and the artist has part of it. And everyone who labors upon the house has part of it. Yet when the palace is completed, is it not worth all it costs? And is the ground upon which it stands not worth more because it is there? And is the ground that adjoins it not worth more because it is there? Wealth grows in magic ways. No man can predict its limits."

"What then, do you advise us to do in order that we may also become rich?" asked still another of his friends. 'We are no longer young men and we have no earnings put aside."

"I advise you to take the wisdom of Aglamish and say to yourselves, 'A part of all I earn is mine to keep.' Say it in the morning when you first arise. Say it at noon. Say it at night. Say it each hour of every day. Say it to yourself until the words stand out like letters of fire across the sky.

"Impress yourself with the idea. Fill yourself with the thought. Then take whatever portion seems wise. Don't make it less than one tenth and put it aside. Arrange your other expenditures to do this if necessary. But lay aside that portion first. Soon you will experience the rich feeling of having something that only you own. As it grows it will stimulate you. A new joy of life will thrill you. You will be motivated to work harder to earn even more. For of your increased earnings, won't the same percentage also be yours to keep?

'Then learn to make your treasure work for you. Make it your slave. Make its children and its children's children work for you.

"Insure an income for your future. Remember that one day you too will be numbered among the aged. Therefore invest your treasure with great caution so that it will not be lost.

"Provide also for your family so that they will not be lacking should you pass away. You can provide such protection by putting aside small payments at regular intervals. The prudent man will not delay in expectation of a large sum becoming available for such a wise purpose.

"Consult with wise men. Seek the advice of men whose daily work is handling money. Let them save you from errors such as those I made myself in entrusting my money to the judgment of Azmur, the brick maker. A small and safe return is far more desirable than a risk.

"Enjoy life while you are here. Don't overstrain or try to save too much. If one tenth of all you earn is as much as you can comfortably keep, be content to keep this portion. Otherwise, live according to your income and don't be afraid to spend. Life is good and life is rich with things worthwhile and things to enjoy."

His friends thanked him and went away. Some were silent because they could not understand. Some were sarcastic because they thought that one so rich should divide his wealth with old friends not as fortunate. But some had a new light in their eyes. They realized that each time Algamish had come back to the room of the scribes he was watching a man work his way out of darkness into light. He was watching a man find a place for himself through his own understanding.

These latter were the ones who, in the following years, frequently revisited Arkad, who received them gladly. He counseled with them and freely gave them of his wisdom, as men of broad experience are always glad to do. And he assisted them in investing their savings so that it would bring in a good interest with safety and would be neither lost nor entangled in investments that paid no dividends.

THE TURNING POINT in these men's lives came the day they realized the truth that had come from Algamish to Arkad, and from Arkad to them.

A Part of All You Earn is Yours to Keep

SEVEN REMEDIES FOR A LEAN PURSE

ROYAL PROCLAMATION

THAT ALL MEN MAY HAVE WEALTH.

Babylon, our beloved city, is the richest in the world, possessing unspoken amounts of gold.

Because a few of our worthy citizens know the laws of wealth, they have grown exceedingly rich. Because many of our citizens do not know the laws of wealth, they remain poor.

Therefore, in order that all my faithful subjects may learn the laws of wealth and be able to acquire gold, I have commanded that the wisdom of the wealthy be taught to all my people.

Be it known that I, your King, have set aside seven days to be devoted to the study of the laws of wealth. Upon the seventeenth day of the first month, I command all my loyal subjects to seek the teachers I have appointed in every part of our city, so that each and all may share justly in the rich treasures of Babylon.

SARGON KING OF BABYLON

THE glory of Babylon endures. Throughout the ages its reputation comes to us as the richest of cities, its treasures as fabulous.

Yet, it was not always so. The riches of Babylon were the results of the money wisdom of its people. They first had to know how to become wealthy.

When the good king, SARGON, returned to Babylon, after defeating his enemies, the Elamites, he was confronted with a serious situation. The royal Chancellor explained it to the king as follows:

"After many years of great prosperity brought to our people because your majesty built the great irrigation canals and the mighty temples to God, now that these works are completed the people seem unable to support themselves.

"The laborers are without employment. The merchants have few customers. The farmers are unable to sell their produce. The people don't have enough gold to buy food."

"But where has all the gold gone that we spent for these great improvements?" demanded the King.

"It has found its way, I fear," responded the Chancellor, "'into the possession of a few very rich men of our city. It filtered through the fingers of most of our people quickly, and now that the stream of gold has ceased to flow, most of our people have nothing to show for their earnings."

The King was thoughtful for some time. Then he asked, "Why should so few men be able to acquire all the gold?"

"Because they know how," replied the Chancellor. "One cannot condemn a man for succeeding because he knows how. Nor can one take away from a man what he has judicially earned, to give to men of lesser ability."

"But why," demanded the King, "should not all the people learn how to accumulate gold and therefore become rich and prosperous themselves?"

"Quite possible, your excellency. But who can teach them? Certainly not the priests, because they know nothing of money making."

"Who in our city knows best how to become wealthy, Chancellor?" asked the King.

"Thy question answers itself, your majesty. Who has amassed the greatest wealth in Babylon?"

"Well said, my able Chancellor. It is Arkad. He is the richest man in Babylon. Bring him to me tomorrow."

The following day, as the King had decreed, Arkad appeared before him, straight and sprightly despite his aging years.

"Arkad," spoke the King, 'is it true that you are the richest man in Babylon?"

"So it is reported, your majesty, and no man denies it."

"How did you become so wealthy?"

'By taking advantage of opportunities available to all citizens of our good city."

'You had nothing to start with?"

"Only a great desire for wealth. Besides this, nothing."

"Arkad," continued the King, "our city is in a very unhappy state because a few know how to acquire wealth and therefore monopolize it, while the mass of our citizens lack the knowledge of how to keep any part of the gold they receive.

"It is my desire that Babylon be the wealthiest city in the world. Therefore, it must be a city of many wealthy men. Therefore, we must teach all the people how to acquire riches. Tell me, Arkad, is there any secret to acquiring wealth? Can it be taught?"

"It is practical, your majesty. What one man knows can be taught to others."

The king's eyes glowed, "Arkad, you speak the very words I wish to hear. Will you lend yourself to this great cause? Will you teach your knowledge to a school for teachers, each of whom will teach others until there are enough trained to teach these truths to every worthy subject in my domain?"

Arkad bowed and said, "I am your humble servant to command. Whatever knowledge I possess, I will gladly give for the betterment of my fellowmen and the glory of my King. Let your good chancellor arrange for me a class of one hundred men and I will teach them the Seven Remedies that fattened my purse, which was once the leanest purse in all of Babylon."

One night later, in compliance with the King's command, the chosen hundred assembled in the great hall of the Temple of Learning, seated upon colorful rugs in a semi-circle. Arkad sat beside them near a smoking lamp that sent forth a strange and pleasing odor.

"There is the richest man in Babylon," whispered a student, nudging his neighbor as Arkad arose. "Yet he is a man just as the rest of us."

"As a dutiful subject of our great King," Arkad began, "I stand before you in his service. Because I was once a poor youth who greatly desired gold, and because I found knowledge that enabled me to acquire it, he asks that I impart my knowledge to you.

"I started my fortune in the humblest way. I had no more advantage that you and every citizen of Babylon enjoy today.

'The first storehouse of my treasure was a well-worn purse. I loathed its useless emptiness. I wanted it to be round and full, clinking with the sound of gold. Therefore, I sought every remedy for a lean purse. I found seven.

"To you, who are assembled before me, I will explain the 'Seven Remedies for a Lean Purse' which I recommend to all men who desire much gold. Each day for seven days, I will explain to you one of the Seven Remedies.

"Listen attentively to the knowledge that I will impart. Debate it with me. Discuss it among yourselves. Learn these lessons thoroughly, so that you may plant in your own purses the seeds of wealth. First, each of you must start to wisely build a fortune of his own. Then, and only then, will you be competent to teach these truths to others.

"I shall teach to you in simple ways how to fatten your purses. This is the first step leading to the temple of wealth, and no man can climb who cannot plant his feet firmly upon the first step.

"We shall now consider the First Remedy."

THE FIRST REMEDY
Start fattening your purse

Arkad addressed a thoughtful man in the second row. "My good friend, what craft do you work at?"

"I," replied the man, "am a scribe and carve records upon the clay tablets."

"I, too, earned my first coppers doing such labor. Therefore, you have the same opportunity to build a fortune."

He spoke to a florid faced man, farther back. "Please tell us what you do to earn your living."

"I," responded this man, "am a meat butcher. I buy goats that the farmers raise, kill them and sell the meat to the housewives, and the hides to the sandal makers."

"Because you also work and earn, you have every advantage to succeed that I had."

In this way, Arkad proceeded to find out how each man labored to earn his living. When he had done questioning them he said:

"Now, my students, you can see that there are many trades at which men can earn coins. Each of the ways of earning is a stream of gold from which the worker can divert a portion to his own purse. Therefore, into each of your purses flows a stream of coins large or small according to each man's ability. Is it not so?"

They all agreed that it was so.

"Then", continued Arkad, "if each one of you desires to build himself a fortune, is it not wise to start by utilizing that source of wealth which he has already established?"

To this they agreed.

Then Arkad turned to a humble man who had declared himself an egg merchant. "If you select one of your baskets and put into it each morning ten eggs and take out from it each evening nine eggs, what will eventually happen?"

"In time it will become overflowing."

"Why?"

"Because each day I put it one more egg than I take out."

Arkad turned to the class with a smile.
"Does any man here have a lean purse?"

First they looked amused. Then they laughed. Lastly they waved their purses in jest.

"All right," he continued, "now I shall tell you the first remedy I learned to cure a lean purse. Do exactly as I have suggested to the egg merchant. For every ten coins you place in your purse, take out but nine for use. Your purse will start to fatten at once and its increasing weight will feel good in your hands and bring satisfaction to your soul.

"Do not ridicule what I say because of its simplicity. The truth is always simple. I told you I would share how I built my fortune. This was my beginning. I, too, carried a lean purse and cursed it because there was nothing in it to satisfy my desires. But when I began to take out from my purse only nine parts out of ten I put in, it began to fatten. So will yours.

"Now I will tell you a strange truth, the reason for which I don't know, but when I started to save one tenth of my earnings, I managed to get along just as well. I was not shorter than before. Also, before long, the coins seemed to come to me more easily than before. Surely it is a law of God that for one who saves and does not spend all of his earnings, gold comes more easily. Likewise, gold avoids one whose purse is empty.

"Which do you desire most? Is it the gratification of your daily desires, a jewel, a bit of finery, better attire, more food; things quickly gone and forgotten? Or is it substantial belongings, gold, lands, herds, merchandise, income that brings investments? The coins you take from your purse bring the first. The coins you leave in your purse will bring the latter.

"This, my students, was the first remedy I discovered for my lean purse: 'For each ten coins I put in, to spend but nine'. Debate this amongst yourselves. If any man proves it untrue, tell me tomorrow when we shall meet again."

THE SECOND REMEDY
Control Your Expenditures

"Some of your members, my students, have asked me this: 'How can a man keep one tenth of all he earns in his purse when all the coins he earns are not enough for his necessary expenses?" Thus Arkad addressed his students on the second day.

"Yesterday, how many of you carried lean purses?"

"All of us," answered the class.

"Yet, you do not all earn the same. Some earn much more than others. Some have much larger families to support. Yet, all purses were equally lean. Now I will tell you an unusual truth about men and sons of men. It is this: That what each of us calls our necessary expenses will always grow to equal our incomes unless we protest to the contrary.

"Do not confuse your necessary expenses with your desires. Each of you, together with your good families, has more desires than your earnings can gratify. Therefore, your earnings are spent to gratify these desires insofar as they will go. And still you might have many ungratified desires.

"All men are burdened with more desires than they can gratify. Because of my wealth, do you think I can gratify every desire? This is a false idea. There are limits to my time. There are limits to my strength. There are limits to the distance I can travel. There are limits to what I can eat. There are limits to the zest with which I can enjoy.

"I say to you that just as weeds grow in a field wherever the farmer leaves space for their roots to take hold, so do desires grow in men whenever there is a possibility of their being gratified. Your desires are many, yet those you can gratify are but few.

"Thoughtfully study your accustomed habits of living – herein are most often found certain accepted expenses that can wisely be reduced or eliminated. Let your motto be 100% of appreciated value demanded for each coin spent.

"Thus, engrave on your clay the things upon which you wish to spend. Select those things that are necessary and those that are possible through the expenditure of nine-tenths of your income. Cross out the rest and consider them but a part of that great multitude of desires that must go unsatisfied and do not regret them.

"Then, budget your necessary expenses. Do not touch the one tenth that is fattening your purse. Let this be your great desire that is being fulfilled. Keep working within your budget; keep adjusting it to help you. Make it your first assistant in defending your fattening purse."

At this point, one of the students, wearing a robe of red and gold, arose and said, "I am a free man. I believe that it is my right to enjoy the good things of life. Therefore I object to the slavery of a budget that determines just how much I may spend and for what. I feel it would remove much pleasure from my life and make me little more than a donkey carrying a burden."

To him Arkad replied. "Who, my friend, will determine your budget?"

"I will make it for myself," responded the protesting one.

"In that case, were a donkey to budget his burden, would he include in it rugs and heavy bars of gold? No. He would include hay and grain and a bag of water for the desert trail.

"The purpose of a budget is to help you fatten your purse. It is to assist you to have your necessities and – insofar as attainable – your other desires. It is to enable you to realize your most cherished desires by defending them from your casual wishes. Like a bright light in a dark cave, your budget shows up the leaks from your purse and enables you to stop them and control your expenditures for definite and gratifying purposes."

"This then is the second remedy for a lean purse. Budget your expenses so that you may have coins to pay for your necessities, to pay for your enjoyments and to gratify your worthwhile desires without spending more than nine-tenths of your earnings."

THE THIRD REMEDY
Make your gold multiply

"Observe your lean purse fattening. You have disciplined yourself to leave in it one-tenth of all you earn. You have controlled your expenditures to protect your growing treasure. Next, we will consider how to put your treasure to labor and increase. Gold in one's purse is gratifying to own and satisfies a miserly soul, but it earns nothing. The gold we retain from our earnings is but the start. The earnings it will make will build our fortunes." So Arkad spoke on the third day to his class.

"How therefore can we put our gold to work? My first investment was unfortunate, for I lost everything. Its story I will tell you later. My first profitable investment was a loan I made to a man named Aggar, a shield maker. Once a year he bought large shipments of bronze from across the sea to use in his trade. Lacking sufficient capital to pay the merchants, he would borrow from those who had extra coins. He was an honorable man. He would pay back what he borrowed, together with an honorable rental, as he sold his shields.

Each time I loaned to him I got back in addition the rental he had paid me. Therefore, not only did my capital increase, but its earnings likewise increased. It was most gratifying to have these sums return to my purse.

I tell you, my students, a man's wealth is not in the coins he carries in his purse; it is in the income he builds, the golden stream that continually flows into his purse and keeps it bulging. That is what every man desires. That is what you, each one of you, desires: an income that continues to come whether you work or travel.

"I have acquired great income; so great that I am called a very rich man. My loans to Aggar were my first training in profitable investment. Gaining wisdom from this experience, I expanded my loans and investments as my capital increased. From a few sources at first, from many sources later, a golden stream of wealth flowed into my purse available for such wise uses as I saw fit.

"See how from my humble earnings, I obtained a hoard of golden slaves, each laboring and earning more gold. As they labored for me, so their children also labored and their children's children until the income from their combined efforts was great.

"Gold increases rapidly when making reasonable earnings, as you will see from the following: A farmer, when his first son was born, took ten pieces of silver to a money lender and asked him to keep it on rental for his son until he became twenty years old. The money lender agreed and set the rental at one-fourth of its value every four years. Because the sum he had set aside belonged to his son, the farmer asked that the rental be added to the principal.

"When the boy reached the age of twenty years, the farmer again went to the money lender to inquire about the silver. The money lender explained that because this sum had increased by compound interest, the original ten pieces of silver had now grown to thirty and a half pieces.

The farmer was very pleased, and since the son did not need the coins, he left them with the money lender. When the son turned fifty years old, the father meantime having passed away, the money lender paid the son in settlement one hundred and sixty seven pieces of silver.

"Thus in fifty years the investment had multiplied itself at rental almost seventeen times.

"This then is the third remedy for a lean purse, to put each coin to laboring so that it can reproduce itself and help bring you income, a stream of wealth that will flow constantly into your purse."

THE FOURTH REMEDY
Guard your treasures from loss

"Misfortune loves a shining mark. Gold in a man's purse must be guarded with firmness, lest it be lost. Thus it is wise that we first secure small amounts and learn to protect them before God entrusts us with larger amounts." So Arkad spoke on the fourth day to his class.

"Every owner of gold is tempted by opportunities that offer the chance to make large sums by its investment in plausible projects. Often friends and relatives are eagerly entering such investments and urge him to follow.

"The first sound principle of investment is security for your principal. Is it wise to be intrigued by larger earnings when your principal may be lost? I say not. The penalty of risk is probable loss. Study each case carefully before parting with your treasure, so that it may be safely reclaimed. Do not be misled by your own romantic desires to make wealth rapidly.

"Before you loan it to any man, assure yourself of his ability to repay and of his reputation for doing so, so that you do not unwittingly hand him your hard earned treasure as a present.

"'Before you entrust it as an investment in any field, acquaint yourself with the dangers it may face.

"My own first investment was a tragedy to me at the time. I entrusted my guarded savings of a year to a brick maker, named Azmur, who was traveling over the far seas to Tyre, where he agreed to buy for me the rare jewels of the Phoenicians. These we were to sell upon his return and divide the profits. The Phoenicians were scoundrels and sold him bits of glass. My treasure was lost. Today, my training allows me to see at once the folly of entrusting a brick maker to buy jewels.

"Therefore, I advise you from the wisdom of my experiences: do not be overly confident in your own wisdom when entrusting your treasures to the possible pitfalls of investments. It is far better to consult the wisdom of those experienced in handling money for profit. Such advice is free for the asking and may readily possess a value equal in gold to the sum you are considering investing. In fact, its value is such if it saves you from loss.

"This then is the fourth remedy for a lean purse, and it is of great importance if it prevents your purse from being emptied once it has become well-filled. Guard your treasure from loss by investing only where your principal is safe, where it may be reclaimed if desired, and where you will not fail to collect a fair rental. Consult with wise men. Secure the advice of men experienced in the profitable handling of gold. Let their wisdom protect you from unsafe investment."

THE FIFTH REMEDY
*Make your home
a profitable investment*

"If a man sets aside nine parts of his earnings upon which to live and enjoy life, and if he can turn any part of this nine parts into a profitable investment without detriment to his well being, then his treasure will grow that much faster." So said Arkad to his class at their fifth lesson.

"All too many of our men of Babylon raise their families in unseemly quarters. They pay high rentals to exacting landlords for small rooms where their wives are unhappy and their children have no place to play except in unclean alleys.

"No man's family can fully enjoy life unless they have a plot of ground where children can play in the clean earth and where the wife can raise good rich herbs to feed her family.

"A man's heart is gladdened when he reaps the crops of his own harvest. To own his house and to have it a place he is proud to care for puts confidence in a man's heart and greater effort behind all his endeavors. Therefore, I recommend that every man own the roof that shelters him and his.

"Nor is it beyond the ability of any well-intentioned man to own his home. Indeed, our great king has widely extended the walls of Babylon so that within them there is much land now unused that can be purchased at most reasonable sums.

"Also, my students, know that money lenders gladly consider the desires of men who seek homes and lands for their families. You may readily borrow to pay the brick maker and the builder for such commendable purposes, if you can show that you yourself have provided a reasonable portion of the necessary sum for the purpose.

"Then when the house is built, you can repay the money lender with the same regularity as you pay the landlord. Since each payment will reduce your indebtedness to the money lender, a few years will pay off his loan.

"Then your heart will be glad because you will own valuable property and your only costs will be the king's taxes.

"Many blessings come to the man who owns his own house. His wife will be happier, and it will greatly reduce his cost of living, making more of his earnings available for pleasures and the gratification of his desires. This then is the Fifth Remedy for a lean purse. Own your own home."

THE SIXTH REMEDY
Insure a future income

'The life of every man proceeds from his childhood to his old age. This is the path of life and no man can deviate from it unless God calls him prematurely to the world beyond. Therefore, I say that it behooves a man to make preparations for a suitable income in the days to come when he is no longer young, and to make preparations for his family to comfort and support them should he no longer be with them. This lesson will instruct you on providing a full purse when time has made you less able to earn." So Arkad addressed his class on the sixth day.

"A man who acquires a growing surplus should give thought to those future days. He should plan certain investments or provisions that will endure safely for many years, yet be available for that time he has so wisely anticipated.

"There are diverse ways by which a man can provide with safety for his future. He might provide a hiding place and bury a secret treasure. Yet, no matter with what skill it is hidden, it may nevertheless become the loot of thieves. For this reason I don't recommend this plan.

"A man may buy houses or lands for this purpose. If wisely chosen as to their usefulness and value in the future, they are permanent in their value, and their earnings or their sale will provide well for his purpose.

"A man may loan a small sum to the money lender and increase it at regular periods. The rental which the money lender adds to this sum will largely add to its increase. I know a sandal maker, named Ansan, who explained to me not long ago that each week for eight years he had deposited with his money lender two pieces of silver. The money lender recently gave him an accounting over which he greatly rejoiced. The total of his small deposits with their rental at the customary rate of one fourth their due for each four years, had now become a thousand and forty pieces of silver.

"I gladly encouraged him further by demonstrating to him with my numerical knowledge that in twelve more years, if he would keep his regular deposits of just two pieces of silver each week, the money lender would then owe him four thousand pieces of silver, a worthy competence for the rest of his life.

"Surely when such a small payment made with regularity produces such profitable results, no man can afford not to insure a treasure for his old age and the protection of his family, no matter how prosperous his business and his investments may be.

"I would like to say more about this. In my mind rests a belief that some day, wise, thinking men will devise a plan to insure men against death whereby many men pay in a trifling sum regularly, the aggregate making a handsome sum for the family of each member who passes away. I see this as something desirable and which I would highly recommend. But today it is not possible because it must reach beyond the life of any man or any partnership to operate. It must be as stable as the King's throne. Some day, I feel that such a plan will come to pass and be a great blessing to many men, because even the first small payment will make a fortune available for the family of a member who passes on.

"But because we live today and not in the days to come, must we take advantage of current means and ways of accomplishing our purposes. Therefore, I recommend to all men, that they, by wise and well thought-out methods, provide against a lean purse in their mature years. For to a man no longer able to earn or to a family without its head, a lean purse is a sore tragedy.

"This then is the Sixth Remedy for a lean Purse. Provide in advance for the needs of your growing age and for the protection of your family."

THE SEVENTH REMEDY
Increase your ability to earn

'Today I will tell you, my students, one of the most vital remedies for a lean purse. Yet, I will not talk of gold but of yourselves, of the men beneath the colorful robes who sit before me. I will talk to you about those things within the minds and lives of men which work for or against their success." So Arkad addressed his class on the seventh day.

"Not long ago a young man came to me asking for a loan. When I asked him why he needed it, he complained that his earnings were insufficient to pay his expenses. I explained to him that this being the case, he was a poor customer for the money lender, as he possessed no surplus earning capacity to repay the loan.

"'What you need, young man', I told him, 'is to earn more coins. What have you done to increase your capacity to earn?

"'All that I can do', he replied. 'I have approached my master six times within two months to request that my pay be increased, but without success. No man can go more often than that.'

"We may smile at his simplicity, yet he did possess one of the vital requirements to increase his earnings. Within him was a strong desire to earn more, a proper and commendable desire.

"Preceding accomplishment must be desire. Your desires must be strong and definite. General desires are but weak longings. For a man to wish to be rich is of little purpose; for a man to desire five pieces of gold is a tangible desire which he can press to fulfillment. After he has backed his desire for five pieces of gold with strength of purpose to secure it, he can then find similar ways to obtain ten pieces and then twenty pieces and later a thousand pieces and behold, he has become wealthy. In learning to secure his one definite, small desire, he has trained himself to secure a larger one. This is the process by which wealth is accumulated:

first in small sums, then in larger ones as a man learns and becomes more capable.

"Desires must be simple and definite. They defeat their own purpose if they are too many, too confusing, or beyond one's training to accomplish.

"As a man perfects himself in his calling, his ability to earn increases. In the days when I was a humble scribe carving upon clay for a few daily coppers, I observed that other workers did more than I did, and were paid more. Therefore, I determined that I would not be exceeded by anyone. Nor did it take long for me to discover the reason for their greater success. More interest in my work, more concentration upon my task, more persistence in my effort, and behold, few men could carve more tablets in a day than I. With reasonable promptness my increased skill was rewarded, and it was unnecessary for me to go six times to my master to request recognition.

'The more wisdom we know, the more we can earn. The man who seeks to learn more of his craft will be richly rewarded. If he is an artisan, he should seek to learn the methods and the tools of those most skillful in the same line. If he labors at the law or at healing, he should consult and exchange knowledge with others of his calling. If he is a merchant, he should continually seek better goods that can be purchased at lower prices.

"The affairs of the world always change and improve because keen-minded men seek greater skill, so that they may better serve those whose patronage they depend upon. Therefore, I urge all men to be in the front rank of progress and not to stand still, lest they be left behind.

"Many things contribute to making a man's life rich with gainful experiences. The following are some of the things a man must do if he wants to respect himself:

"He must pay his debts promptly, not purchasing what he is unable to pay for.

45

"He must take care of his family so that they think and speak well of him.

"He must make a will of record so that in case God calls him, proper and honorable division of his property can take place.

"He must have compassion for those who are injured or smitten by misfortune and help them within reasonable limits. He must perform thoughtful deeds to those who are dear to him.

"Thus the seventh and last remedy for a lean purse is to cultivate your powers, to study and become wiser, to become more skillful, to act so as to respect yourself. Thereby, you will acquire confidence in yourself to achieve your carefully considered desires.

'These then are the Seven Remedies for a Lean Purse, which, out of my experience of a long and successful life, I urge for all men who desire wealth.

"There is MORE GOLD in BABYLON, my students, than you can dream of. There is abundance for all.

"Go forth and practice these truths so that you may prosper and grow wealthy, as is your right.

"Go forth and teach these truths so that every honorable subject of his majesty may also share liberally in the ample wealth of our beloved city. THIS IS YOUR KING'S COMMAND!"

THE DEBATE OF GOOD LUCK

THE Temple of Learning in old Babylon was an unusual institution. In this spacious building many groups of men would congregate each evening about their favorite leaders to discuss interesting subjects.

Within the doors of this temple all men met as equals. Here the humblest slave could converse upon an equal footing with a prince of the royal house.

When Arkad arrived at his special corner on a certain evening, forty men reclining on small rugs were awaiting him.

"What shall we discuss tonight?" inquired Arkad.

"I have a subject," ventured a tall cloth weaver, arising as was the custom. "'Today I am lucky, for I found a purse with pieces of gold. I wish to continue to be lucky. Feeling that all men share this desire with me, I suggest we debate *good luck*. Let us try to discover if there are ways luck can be enticed to someone."

"A most interesting subject has been suggested to us," Arkad resumed. 'To some, good luck is a chance happening that can come to any man. Others believe that the instigator of all good fortune is 'good luck', which is attracted to a favored few. What do you say, my friends – shall we attempt to discover if there are means by which good luck may be enticed to visit each and all of us?"

"Yes! Yes!" responded his listeners.

"To seek good luck requires action on our part. Who can offer a suggestion as to where we should begin our search?" queried Arkad.

"That I will do," spoke a well-robed youth, arising. "When a man speaks of luck is it not natural that his thoughts turn to the gaming tables? Is it not there that we find many men courting good luck in the hope that it will favor them with rich winnings?"

"Continue your story," called a voice as he resumed his seat. "Did you find good luck there?"

"I must admit it didn't seem to know that I was there," he replied "How about you? Have you found luck awaiting you in such places?"

"A wise start," broke in Arkad. "We meet here to consider all sides of each question. To ignore the gaming tables would be to pass by an instinct quite common in most men, the love of taking a chance with the hope of winning."

"That reminds me of the races yesterday", called another man. "If luck frequents the gaming tables, certainly it doesn't overlook the races, which, to me, are far more pleasurable. Tell us, Arkad, was it good luck that whispered to you to bet upon those greys from Nineveh? I stood right behind when you placed your bet and could scarce believe my ears, good as they are. You know as well as all of us that no team can beat our beloved bays. Does it not look as though good luck whispered in your ear that the inside black was to stumble as they made the last turn, and trip the bays to give the greys an unearned victory?"

Arkad smiled good-humoredly at the banter. "What reasons do we have to think that luck would take that much interest in any man's bet on a horse race? Nor do I find good luck at the gaming tables where men lose more gold they can win.

"In honest trading such as buying and selling, a man can expect to make a profit on his transactions. (Perhaps not on all because sometimes he acts without good judgment). But if he persists he can usually expect to make his profit. This is so because the chance of profit is always in his favor.

"But when a man plays the games, the chance of profit is always against him and always in favor of the game keeper. The game is arranged to favor the keeper. It is his business at which he plans to make a large profit for himself. Few men realize how certain the game keeper's profit is and how poor their own chances are to win.

"Thus for an example let us consider betting on dice. Each time the cube is cast we bet which side will be uppermost. If it's the red side, the game master pays us four times our bet. If any one of the other five sides shows uppermost, we lose. Thus the figures show that for each cast the player has five chances to lose, and because the red pays four to one, he has four chances to win. In a night's play the game master expects to keep for himself one fifth of all the wagers made. Can any man expect to win consistently against such odds, arranged so that he will lose consistently?"

"Yet some men do win large sums at times," volunteered one of the listeners.

"Quite so, they do," Arked continued. "Realizing this, I have often wondered whether money secured in such ways brings any worthwhile value to those who receive it. Many of the successful men of Babylon are among my acquaintances, yet I cannot name one of them who can trace his start to such a source. You who are here tonight must know a great many more of the substantial citizens of our city. To me it would be of interest to learn how many of our better citizens can credit the gaming tables with their start or their support. What do you say?"

There was a prolonged pause. Finally a voice enquired, "Would your enquiry include the game keeper?"

"If not one of you can think of anyone else. But wait, how about yourselves? Are there any consistent winners with us here who hesitate to advise us about the sources of their incomes?"

His challenge was answered by a loud groan from the rear taken up and spread by others amid much laughter. "It would appear we are searching far from where we should.

"Who among you has at any time had good luck such as our friend,

49

the cloth weaver, finding gold or valuables? What, no one? Then, rare indeed is this kind of good luck. Who among you has had good luck within your reach only to let it escape?"

Many hands were raised. "Speak up one of you! Let us hear how it could escape you. Who wants to be first?"

An elderly merchant arose, smoothing his genteel white robes. "With your permission, most honorable Arkad, and friends, I will gladly relate a tale that illustrates how close good luck can come to a man and how he can blindly permit it to escape, much to his loss.

"Many years ago when I was a young man, just married and beginning to earn, my father come one day and urged me most strongly to enter an investment. The son of one of his good friends had taken notice of a barren tract of land not far beyond the outer walls of our city. It lay high above the canal where no water could reach it.

"The son of my father's friend devised a plan to purchase this land, build three large water wheels that could be operated by oxen and thereby raise the life-giving waters to the fertile soil. This accomplished, he planned to divide the land into small tracts and sell them to the residents of the city for herb patches.

"The son of my father's friend did not possess sufficient gold to complete such an undertaking. Like myself, he was a young man earning a fair sum. His father, like mine, was a man of large family and small means. He, therefore, decided to interest a group of men to enter the enterprise with him. The group was to comprise twelve, each of whom must be a money earner and agree to pay one tenth of his earnings into the enterprise until the land was made ready for sale. All would then share justly in the profits in proportion to their investment.

'You, my son', my father said to me, 'are now in your young manhood. It is highly desirable that you begin building a valuable estate for yourself so that you will become respected among men.'

"This I most ardently desire, my father," I replied.

"'Then, do as I advise. Do what I should have done at your age. From your earnings, keep one tenth aside to put into favorable investments. With this one tenth of your earnings and what it will also earn, you can accumulate for yourself a valuable estate, even before you reach my age'.

"Your words are words of wisdom, my father. I greatly desire riches. Yet I need my earnings for many uses. Therefore, I hesitate to do as you advise. I am young. There is plenty of time'.

"'So I thought at your age, yet behold, many years have passed and I have not yet made the beginning'.

"We live in a different age, my father, I will avoid your mistakes".

"'Opportunity stands before you, my son. It is offering a chance that may lead to wealth. I beg of you not to delay. Go tomorrow to the son of my friend and bargain with him to pay ten percent of your earnings into this investment. Go promptly tomorrow. Opportunity waits for no man. Today it is here; soon it is gone. Therefore, do not delay!'

"In spite of the advice of my father, I did hesitate. There were beautiful new robes just brought by the tradesmen from the East, robes of such richness and beauty, my good wife and I felt we must each possess one. Should I agree to pay one tenth of my earnings into the enterprise, we would have to deprive ourselves of these and other pleasures we dearly desired. I delayed making a decision until it was too late, much to my subsequent regret. The enterprise proved to be more profitable than any man had prophesied. This is my tale, showing how I permitted good luck to escape."

"In this tale we see how *good luck comes to that man who accepts opportunity,*" commented a swarthy man of the desert. "There must always be a starting place for the building of an estate. That start may be a few pieces of gold or silver which a man diverts from his earnings to his first investment. I, myself, am the owner of many herds. The start of my herds began when I was a mere boy and when I purchased a young calf with one piece of silver. This beginning of my wealth was of great importance to me.

'To take one's first step in building an estate is as much good luck as can come to any man. With all men, that first step, which changes them from men who earn from their own labor to men who draw dividends from the earnings of their gold, is important. Some, fortunately, take it when they are young and thereby financially outstrip those who take it later or those unfortunate men like the father of this merchant who never take it at all.

"Had our friend, the merchant, taken this step in his early manhood when this opportunity came to him, today he would be blessed with much more of this world's goods. Should the good luck of our friend, the cloth weaver, cause him to take such a step at this time, it will indeed be but the beginning of much greater good fortune."

"'Thank you! I like to speak, also." A stranger from another country arose. "I am a Syrian. Not so well do I speak your tongue. I wish to call this friend, the merchant, a name. Maybe you think it not polite, this name. Yet I wish to call him that. But, alas, I not know your word for it. If I do call it in Syrian, you will not understand. Therefore, please some good gentlemen, tell me that right name you call man who puts off doing those things that mighty good for him."

"Procrastinator," called a voice.

'That's him," shouted the Syrian, waving his hands excitedly, "he accepts not opportunity when she comes. He waits. He says I have much business right now. By and by I talk to you. Opportunity, she will not wait for such slow fellow. She thinks if a man desires to be lucky he will step quick. Any man who not step quick when opportunity comes, he big procrastinator like our friend, this merchant."

The merchant arose and bowed good-naturedly in response to the laughter. "I admire this stranger within our gates, who does not hesitate to speak the truth."

"And now let us hear another tale of opportunity. Who has another experience for us?" demanded Arkad.

"I have," responded a red-robed man of middle age. "I am a buyer of animals, mostly camels and horses. Sometimes I also buy sheep and goats. The tale I am about to relate will truthfully tell how opportunity came one night when I least expected it. Perhaps this is the reason I let it escape. You will be the judge of this.

"Returning to the city one evening after a disheartening ten day journey in search of camels, I was angry to find the gates of the city closed and locked. While my slaves spread our tent for the night, which we had to pass with little food and no water, I was approached by an elderly farmer who also found himself locked out.

'Honored sir', he addressed me, 'from your appearance I judge you to be a buyer. If so, I would very much like to sell to you the most excellent flock of sheep just driven up. Alas, my good wife lies very sick with fever. I must return to her quickly. Won't you buy my sheep so that I and my slaves can mount our camels and travel back without delay'?

"It was so dark I could not see his flock, but from the bleating I knew it must be large. Having wasted ten days searching for camels I could not find, I was glad to bargain with him. In his anxiety, he set a most reasonable price. I accepted, well knowing my slaves could drive the flock through the city gates in the morning and sell them at a substantial profit.

"Having concluded the bargain, I called my slaves to bring torches so that we might count the flock which the farmer declared to contain nine hundred. I will not burden you, my friends, with a description of our difficulty in trying to count so many thirsty, restless, milling sheep. It proved to be an impossible task.

Therefore, I bluntly informed the farmer I would count them at daylight and pay him then.

'Please, most honorable sir', he pleaded. 'Pay me but two thirds of the price tonight so that I may be on my way. I will leave my most intelligent and educated slave to assist you in counting in the morning. He is trustworthy and you can pay him the balance'.

"But I was stubborn and refused to make payment that night. The next morning, before I awoke, the city gates opened and four buyers rushed out in search of flocks. They were most eager and willing to pay high prices because the city was threatened with siege, and food was scarce. The farmer received nearly three times the price he had offered me for the flock. This is how rare good luck was allowed to escape."

"Here is a most unusual tale," commented Arkad. "What wisdom does it suggest?"

"The wisdom of making a payment immediately when we are convinced our bargain is wise," suggested a venerable saddle maker. "If the bargain is good, then you need protection against your own weaknesses as much as against any other man. We mortals are changeable and alas are apt to change our minds. We are stubborn indeed, and we are prone to vacillate and let opportunity escape. My first judgment is my best. Yet I have always found it difficult to compel myself to proceed with a good bargain when made. Therefore, as a protection against my own weaknesses, I make a prompt deposit right there and then. This saves me from later regrets for the good luck that should have been mine."

"Thank you! Again I like to speak." The Syrian was upon his feet once more. 'These tales much alike. Each time opportunity fly away for same reason. Each time she come to *procrastinator*, bringing good plan. Each time they hesitate, not say, right now best time, I do it quick. How can men succeed that way?"

"Your words are wise, my friend," responded the buyer. "Good luck fled from procrastination in both these tales. Yet, this is not unusual. The spirit of procrastination is within all men. We desire riches; yet, how often when opportunity appears before us, that spirit of procrastination from within urges various delays in our acceptance. *In listening to it we become our own worst enemies.*

"In my younger days I didn't know it by this long word our friend from Syria enjoys. At first I thought it was my poor judgment that caused me loss of many profitable trades. Later, I credited it to my stubborn disposition. At last, I recognized it for what it was – a habit of needless delaying where action was required, prompt and decisive action. How I hated it when its true character stood revealed. With bitterness, I broke loose from this enemy to my success."

'Thank you! I like ask question from Mr. Merchant." The Syrian was speaking. "You wear fine robes, not like those of poor man. You speak like successful man. Tell us, do you listen now when procrastination whispers in your ear?"

"Like our friend the buyer, I also had to recognize and conquer procrastination," responded the merchant. "To me, it proved to be an enemy, ever watching and waiting to thwart my accomplishments. The tale I related is but one of many similar instances I could tell to show how it drove away my opportunities. It is not difficult to conquer, once understood. *No man willingly permits a thief to rob him of his grain. Nor does any man willingly permit an enemy to drive away his customers and rob him of his profits.* Once I recognized the acts my enemy was committing, I conquered it with determination. So every man must master his own spirit of procrastination before he can expect to share in the rich treasures of Babylon.

"What do you say, Arkad? Since you are the richest man in Babylon, many proclaim you to be the luckiest. Do you agree with me that no man can arrive at a full measure of success until he has completely crushed the spirit of procrastination within him?

"It is as you say," Arkad admitted. "During my long life I have watched generation following generation, marching forward along those avenues of trade, science and learning that lead to success in life. Opportunities came to all these men. Some grasped theirs and moved steadily to the gratification of their deepest desires, but the majority hesitated, faltered and fell behind."

Arkad turned to the cloth weaver. 'You suggested that we debate good luck. Let us hear what you think now about the subject."

"I see good luck in a different light. I had thought of it as something most desirable that might happen to a man without effort on his part. Now, I realize such happenings are not the sort of thing one may attract to himself. *From our discussion have I learned that to attract good luck to oneself, it is necessary to take advantage of opportunities.* Therefore, in the future I will endeavor to make the best of such opportunities as they come to me."

"You have grasped well the truths brought forth in our discussion," Arkad replied. "Good
luck, we find, often follows opportunity but seldom comes otherwise. Our merchant friend would have found great good luck had he accepted the opportunity the good goddess presented to him. Our friend the buyer, likewise, would have enjoyed good luck had he completed the purchase of the flock and sold it at a handsome profit.

"We pursued this discussion to find a means by which good luck could be enticed to us. I feel that we have found the way. Both tales illustrated how good luck follows opportunity. Herein lies a truth that many similar tales of good luck, won or lost, could not change. The truth is this: Good luck can be enticed by accepting opportunity.

'Those eager to grasp opportunities for their betterment attract 'good luck'. It seems to favor men of action best. Therefore, if a plan is in your best interest, promptly accept it. If it is against your best interest, with equal promptness, reject it.

"ACTION will lead you forward to the successes you desire."

Men of Action are favored by Good Luck

THE TALE OF THE FIVE LAWS OF GOLD

"A BAG heavy with gold or a clay tablet carved with words of wisdom: if you had your choice, which would you choose?"

By the flickering light from the fire of desert shrubs, the suntanned faces of his listeners gleamed with interest.

"The GOLD, the GOLD," chorused the twenty-seven.

Old Kalabab smiled knowingly.

"Hark," he resumed, raising his hand. "Hear the wild dogs out there in the night. They howl and wail because they are lean with hunger. Yet feed them, and what do they? Fight and strut. Then fight and strut some more, giving no thought to tomorrow that will surely come.

"So it is with the sons of men. Give them a choice of gold and wisdom – what do they do? Ignore the wisdom and waste the gold. The next day they wail because they have no more gold.

"Gold is reserved for those who know its laws and abide by them."

Kalabab drew his white robe close about his lean legs, for a cool night wind was blowing.

"Because you have served me faithfully upon our long journey, because you cared well for my camels, because you toiled uncomplainingly across the hot sands of the desert, because you fought bravely the robbers that sought to despoil my merchandise, I will tell you tonight the tale of the 'FIVE LAWS OF GOLD', a tale as you have never heard before."

"Listen attentively to the words I speak, for if you grasp their meaning and heed them, in the days that come you will have much gold."

He paused impressively. Above in a canopy of blue, the stars shone brightly in the crystal
clear skies of Babylonia. Behind the group their faded tents loomed tightly staked against possible desert storms. Beside the tents were neatly stacked bales of merchandise covered with skins. Nearby the camel herd sprawled in the sand, some chewing their cuds contentedly, others snoring in hoarse discord.

"You have told us many good tales, Kalabab" spoke up the chief packer "We look to your wisdom to guide us tomorrow when our service with you will be at an end."

"I have told you of my adventures in strange and distant lands, but tonight I will tell you of the wisdom of Arkad, the wise rich man."

"We have we heard much about him," edged the chief packer, "for he was the richest man that ever lived in Babylon."

"The richest man he was, because he was wise in the ways of gold as no man had ever been before him. Tonight I will tell of his great wisdom as it was told to me by Nomasir his son, many years ago in Nineveh, when I was but a lad.

"My master and myself had tarried long into the night in the palace of Nomasir. I had helped my master bring great bundles of fine rugs, each one to be tried by Nomasir until his choice of colors was satisfied. At last he was pleased and commanded us to sit with him and to drink a rare vintage odorous to the nostrils and most warming to my stomach, which was unaccustomed to such a drink. Then, he told us this tale of the great wisdom of Arkad, his father, as I will tell it to you.

"In Babylon it is the custom, as you know, that the sons of wealthy fathers live with their parents in expectation of inheriting the estate. Arkad did not approve of this custom. Therefore, when young Nomasir reached the man's estate, he sent for the young man and addressed him:

"'My son, it is my desire that you inherit my estate. However, you must first prove that you are capable of handling it wisely. Therefore, I want you to go out into the world and show your ability both to acquire gold, and to make yourself respected among men.

"'To start you well, I will give you two things that I, myself, was denied when I started as a poor youth to build a fortune.

"'First, I give you this bag of gold. If you use it wisely, it will be the basis of your future success.

"'Second, I give you this clay tablet upon which are carved "THE FIVE LAWS OF GOLD." If you apply them in your own acts, they will bring you competence and security.

"'Ten years from this day, come back to the house of your father and give an account of yourself. If you prove worthy, I will then make you the heir to my estate. Otherwise, I will give it to the priests so that they can barter the kind consideration of God for my soul.

"So Nomasir went forth to make his own way, taking his bag of gold, the clay tablet carefully wrapped in silken cloth, his slave and the horses upon which they rode.

"The ten years passed, and Nomasir, as he had agreed, returned to his father who provided a great feast in his honor, to which he invited many friends and relatives. After the feast was over, the father and mother mounted their throne-like seats at one side of the great hall, and Nomasir stood before them to give an account of himself as he had promised his father.

"It was evening. The room was hazy with smoke from the wicks of the oil lamps that dimly lit it. Slaves in white woven jackets and tunics fanned the humid air rhythmically with long stemmed palm leaves. A stately dignity colored the scene. Nomasir's wife and his two young sons, along with friends and other members of the family, sat upon rugs behind him, eager listeners.

"'My father," he began deferentially, "'I bow before your wisdom. Ten years ago when I stood at the gates of manhood, you bade me to go forth and become a man among men, instead of remaining a vassal to your fortune.

"'You gave me liberally of your gold. You gave me liberally of your wisdom. Of the gold, alas! I must admit I handled it disastrously. It fled, indeed, from my inexperienced hands at the first opportunity.

The father smiled indulgently. 'Continue, my son, your tale interests me in all its details.'

"'I decided to go to Nineveh, as it was a growing city, believing that I might find opportunities there. I joined a caravan and among its members made numerous friends. Two well-spoken men who had a most beautiful white horse as fleet as the wind, were among these.

"'As we journeyed, they told me in confidence that in Nineveh there was a wealthy man who owned a horse so swift that it had never been beaten. Its owner believed that no living horse could run with greater speed. Therefore, he would bet any sum however large that his horse could outrun any horse in all Babylonia. Compared to their horse, my friends said, it was but a lumbering ass that could be beaten with ease.

"'They offered, as a great favor, to permit me to join them in a wager. I was quite carried away with the plan.

"'Our horse was badly beaten and I lost much of my gold.' The father laughed. "Later, I discovered that this was a deceitful plan and that these men constantly journeyed with caravans seeking victims. You see, the man in Nineveh was their partner and shared with them the bets he won. This shrewd deceit taught me my first lesson in looking out for myself.

"'I was soon to learn another, equally bitter. In the caravan there was another young man with whom I became quite friendly. He was the son of wealthy parents and like myself, was journeying to Nineveh to find a suitable location. Not long after our arrival, he told me that a merchant had died and his shop with its rich merchandise and patronage could be secured at a paltry price. Saying that we would be equal partners, but that he must first return to Babylon to secure his gold, he prevailed upon me to purchase the stock with my gold, agreeing that his would be used later to carry on our venture.

"'He delayed the trip to Babylon for a long time, proving in the meantime to be an unwise buyer and a foolish spender. I finally put him out, but not before the business had deteriorated to where we had only poor goods and no gold to buy other goods. I sacrificed what was left to an Israelite for a pitiful sum.

"'I tell you, my father, bitter days followed. I sought employment and found none, for I had no trade or training that would enable me to earn. I sold my horses. I sold my slave. I sold my extra robes so that I would have food and a place to sleep, but each day was grimmer.

"'But in those bitter days, I remembered your confidence in me, my father. You sent me forth to become a man, and I was determined to accomplish this.' The mother buried her face and wept softly.

"'At this time, I remembered the tablet you had given to me on which you had carved "THE FIVE LAWS OF GOLD." Thereupon, I read your words of wisdom most carefully, and realized that had I sought wisdom first, my gold would not have been lost to me. I learned each law by heart, determined that when the goddess of good fortune smiled upon me once more, I would be guided by the wisdom of age and not by the inexperience of youth.

"'For the benefit of you who are seated here tonight, I will read my father's wisdom as engraved upon the clay tablet which he gave me ten years ago.'

THE FIVE LAWS OF GOLD

I. Gold comes gladly and in increasing quantity to any man who will put by not less than one-tenth of his earnings to create an estate for his future and that of his family.

II. Gold labors diligently and contentedly for the wise owner who finds profitable employment for it, multiplying as the flocks of the field.

III. Gold clings to the protection of the cautious owner who invests it under the advice of men wise in its handling.

IV. Gold slips away from the man who invests it in businesses or purposes with which he is not familiar or which are not approved by those skilled in its keep.

V. Gold flees the man who would force it to impossible earnings or who follows the alluring advice of tricksters and schemers or who trusts it to his own inexperience and romantic desires in investment.

"'These are the five laws of gold as written by my father. I proclaim them as having greater value than gold itself, as I will show by the continuance of my tale."

"He again faced his father. 'I have told you of the depth of poverty and despair to which my experience brought me.

"'However there is no chain of disasters that will not come to an end. Mine came when I secured employment managing a crew of slaves working upon the new outer wall of the city.

"'Profiting from my knowledge of the first law of gold, I saved a copper from my first earnings, adding to it at every opportunity until I had a piece of silver. It was a slow procedure, for one must live. I spent grudgingly, I admit, because I was determined to earn back as much gold as you, my Father, had given to me, before the ten years were over.

"'One day the slave master with whom I had become quite friendly, said to me: "You are a thrifty youth who doesn't spend wantonly what he earns. Have you any gold put aside that is not earning?"

"Yes", I replied, "it is my greatest desire to accumulate gold to replace that which my father gave to me and which I have lost."

"'This a worthy ambition, I will grant, and do you know that the gold which you have saved can work for you and earn much more gold?"

"'Alas! My experience has been bitter, for my father's gold has fled me, and I am afraid lest my own gold does the same".

"If you have confidence in me, I will give you a lesson in the profitable handling of gold," he replied. "Within a year the outer wall will be complete and ready for the great gates of bronze that will be built at each entrance to protect the city from the king's enemies. In all Nineveh there is not enough metal to make these gates and the king has not thought to provide it. Here is my plan: A group of us will pool our gold and send a caravan to the mines of copper and tin, which are distant, and bring to Nineveh the metal for the gates. When the king says, 'Make the great gates', we alone will be able to supply the metal and the king will pay a rich price. If the king will not buy from us, we will still have the metal which can be sold for a fair price."

"'In his offer I recognized an opportunity to abide by the third law and invest my savings under the guidance of wise men. Nor was I disappointed. Our pool was a success, and my small store of gold was greatly increased by the transaction.

"'In due time, I was accepted as a member of this same group in other ventures. They were men wise in the profitable handling of gold. They talked over each plan presented with great care, before entering upon it. They would take no chance on losing their principal or tying it up in unprofitable investments from which their gold could not be recovered. Such foolish things as the horse race and the partnership into which I had entered with my inexperience, would have had scant consideration with them. They would have immediately pointed out their weaknesses.

"'Through my association with these men, I learned to safely invest gold to bring profitable returns. As the years went on, my treasure increased more and more rapidly. I not only made back as much as I lost, but much more.

"'Through my misfortunes, my trials and my success, I have tested time and again the wisdom of the Five Laws of Gold, my father, and have proven them true in every test. To one who is without knowledge of the Five Laws, Gold comes rarely, and goes away quickly. But to one who abides by the Five Laws, Gold comes and works as his dutiful Slave."

Nomasir stopped speaking and motioned to a slave in the back of the room. The slave brought forward, one at a time, three heavy leather bags. One of these Nomasir took and placed on the floor before his father addressing him again:

"You gave me a bag of gold, Babylon gold. Behold in its place, I return to you a bag of Nineveh gold of equal weight. An equal exchange as all will agree.

"You gave me a clay tablet inscribed with wisdom. Behold, in its stead, I return two bags of gold." So saying, he took from the slave the other two bags and, likewise, placed them on the floor before his father.

"I do this to prove to you, my father, how much more valuable I consider your wisdom than your gold. Yet, who can measure in bags of gold, the value of wisdom? Without wisdom, gold is quickly lost by those who have it, but with wisdom, gold can be secured by those who don't have it, as these three bags of gold prove.

"It gives me the deepest satisfaction, my father, to stand before you and say that, because of your wisdom, I have been able to become rich and respected before men."

The father placed his hand fondly on Nomasir's head. "You have learned your lessons well, and I am, indeed, fortunate to have a son to whom I may entrust my wealth."

Kalabab ceased his tale and looked critically at his listeners.

"What does this tale of Nomasir mean to you?" he continued.

"Who among you can go to your father or to your wife's father and give an account of the wise handling of his earnings?"

"What would these venerable men think were you to say, 'I have traveled a lot and learned a lot and labored a lot and earned a lot, yet alas, I have little gold. Some I spent wisely, and some I spent foolishly and much I lost in unwise ways'.

"Do you still think that it's an inconsistency of fate that some men have much gold and others have none? Then you err.

"Men have much gold when they know the Five Laws of Gold and abide by them.

"Because I learned these Five Laws in my youth and abided by them, I have become a wealthy merchant. I did not accumulate my wealth by some strange magic.

"Wealth that comes quickly goes the same way.

"Wealth that stays to give enjoyment and satisfaction to its owner, comes gradually, because it is a child born of knowledge and persistent purpose.

"To earn wealth is only a slight burden to the thoughtful man. Bearing the burden consistently from year to year accomplishes the final purpose.

"The Five Laws of Gold offer you rich reward for their observance.

"Each of these Five Laws is rich with meaning and lest you overlook this in the briefness of my tale, I will now repeat them. I know each of them by heart because in my youth, I could see their value and would not be content until I knew them word for word."

The First Law

Gold comes gladly and in increasing quantity to any man who will put by not less than one-tenth of his earnings to create an estate for his future and that of his family.

"Any man who puts by one-tenth of his earnings consistently and invests it wisely will create a valuable estate that will provide an income for him in the future and further guarantee safety for his family in case God calls him to the world of darkness. This law also says that gold comes gladly to such a man. I can truly certify this in my own life. The more gold I accumulate, the more readily it comes to me and in increased quantities. The gold which I save earns more, as yours will, and its earnings earn more, and this is the working out of the first law."

The Second Law of Gold

Gold labors diligently and contentedly for the wise owner who finds profitable employment for it, multiplying as the flocks of the field.

"Gold, indeed, is a willing worker. It is ever eager to multiply when opportunity presents itself. To every man who has a store of gold set by, opportunity comes for its most profitable use. As the years pass, it multiplies itself in surprising fashion."

The Third Law of Gold

Gold clings to the protection of the cautious owner who invests it under the advice of men wise in its handling.

"Gold, indeed, clings to the cautious owner, even as it flees the careless owner. The man who seeks the advice of men wise in handling gold, soon learns not to jeopardize his treasure, but to preserve it in safety and to enjoy its consistent increase in contentment."

The Fourth Law of Gold

Gold slips away from the man who invests it in businesses or purposes with which he not familiar or which are not approved by those skilled in its keep.

"To the man who has gold, yet is not skilled in its handling, many uses for it appear most profitable. Too often these are fraught with danger of loss, and if properly analyzed by wise men, show small possibility of profit. Therefore, the inexperienced owner of gold who trusts his own judgment and invests it in business or purposes with which he is not familiar, too often finds his judgment imperfect, and pays with his treasure for his inexperience. Wise indeed, is he who invests his treasures under the advice of men skilled in the ways of gold."

The Fifth Law of Gold

Gold flees the man who would force it to impossible earnings or who follows the alluring advice of tricksters and schemers or who trusts it to his own inexperience and romantic desires in its investment.

"Fanciful propositions that thrill like adventure tales always come to the new owner of gold. These appear to endow his treasure with magic powers that will enable it to make impossible earnings. Yet heed the wise men for they know the risks that lurk behind every plan to make great wealth suddenly.

"Do not forget the rich men of Nineveh who would take no chance of losing their principal or tying it up in unprofitable investments.

"This ends my tale of 'The Five Laws of Gold.' In telling it to you, I have shared with you the secrets of my own success.

"'Yet, they are not secrets but truths which every man who wishes to step out of the multitude must first learn and then follow.

"Tomorrow, we enter Babylon. Look! See the fire that eternally burns above the Temple of Bel! We are already in sight of the golden city. Tomorrow, each of you will have gold, the gold you have so well earned by your faithful services.

"Ten years from this night, what will you tell about this gold?

"If there are men among you, who, like Nomasir, will use a portion of their gold to start for themselves an estate and be wisely guided by the wisdom of Arkad, ten years from now – it's a safe wager – like the son of Arkad, they will be rich and respected among men.

"Our wise acts accompany us through life to please us and to help us. Just as surely, our unwise acts follow us to plague and torment us. Alas, they cannot be forgotten. In the front rank of the torments that follow us are the memories of the things we should have done, of the opportunities which came to us and which we did not take.

"Rich are the Treasures of Babylon, so rich that no man can count their value in pieces of gold. Each year, they grow richer and more valuable. Like the treasures of every land, they are a reward, a rich reward awaiting those men of purpose who are determined to secure their just share.

"In the strength of your desires is a magic power. Guide this power with your knowledge of 'The Five Laws of Gold' and you will share in the Treasures of Babylon."

THE TALE OF THE GOLD LENDER OF BABYLON

FIFTY PIECES OF GOLD! Never before had Rodan, the spear maker of old Babylon, carried so much gold in his leather wallet. He strode happily down the king's highway from the palace of his most liberal Majesty. Cheerfully the gold clinked as the wallet at his belt swayed with each step the sweetest music he had ever heard.

Fifty pieces of gold! All his! He could hardly believe his good fortune. What power in those clinking discs! They could purchase anything he wanted, a grand house, land, cattle, camels, horses, chariots, whatever he might desire.

For what should he use it? That evening as he turned into a side street towards his sister's home, he could think of nothing he would rather possess than those same glittering, heavy pieces of gold – his to keep.

It was upon an evening some days later that a perplexed Rodan entered the shop of Mathon, the lender of gold and dealer in jewels and rare fabrics. Glancing neither to the right nor the left at the colorful articles artfully displayed, he passed through to the living quarters at the rear. Here he found the genteel Mathon lounging upon a rug partaking of a
meal served by a black slave.

"I want to counsel with you for I don't know what to do." Rodan stood stolidly, feet apart, hairy breast exposed by the gaping front of his leather jacket.

Mathon's narrow, sallow face smiled a friendly greeting. "What indiscretions do you have that you seek the lender of gold? Have you been unlucky at the gaming table? Or has some dame entangled you? I have known you for many years, yet never before have you asked me to help you with your troubles."

"No, no – nothing like that. I don't seek gold. Instead I wish for your wise advice."

"Hear! Hear! What do you say? No one comes to the lender of gold for advice. My ears must be deceiving me."

"They hear correctly."

"Can this be so? Rodan, the spear maker, who displays more cunning than all the rest, comes to Mathon, not for gold, but for advice. Many men come to me for gold to pay for their follies, but as for advice, they don't want any. Yet who is more able to advise than the lender of gold to whom many men come in trouble?

"You will eat with me, Rodan," he continued. "You will be my guest for the evening. Ando!" he commanded of the black slave, "draw up a rug for my friend, Rodan the spear maker, who comes for advice. He will be my honored guest. Bring him lots of food and get him my largest cup. Choose the best wine so that he may enjoy drinking.

"Tell me what troubles you."

"It is the king's gift."

"The king's gift? The king gave you a gift and it troubles you? What manner of gift?"

"Since he was so pleased with the design I submitted to him for a new point on the spears of the royal guard, he presented me with fifty pieces of gold, and now I am perplexed. I am sought out each hour of the day by those who want to share it with me."

"That is natural. More men want gold than have it, and wish the one who comes by it to easily divide. But can you not say 'No'? Is your will not as strong as your fist?"

'To many I can say no, yet sometimes it would be easier to say yes. Can one refuse to share with one's only sister to whom he is deeply devoted?"

"Surely, your sister would not wish to deprive you of enjoying your reward."

"But it is for the sake of Araman, her husband, whom she wishes to see a rich merchant.
She feels that he has never had a chance and she begs me to loan to him this gold so that he may become a prosperous merchant and repay me from his profits."

"My friend," resumed Mathon, "you bring a worthy subject to discuss. Gold brings to its possessor responsibility and a changed position with his fellow men. It brings fear lest he lose it or it be tricked away from him. It brings a feeling of power and the ability to do good. Likewise, it brings opportunities whereby his very good intentions can lead him into difficulties. Did you ever hear of the farmer of Nineveh who could understand the language of animals? I will tell it to you, for you should know that there is more than the passing of gold from the hands of one to the hands of another when borrowing and lending.

"This farmer who could understand what the animals said to each other, lingered in the farmyard each evening just to listen to their words. One evening he heard the ox bemoaning to the ass about the hardness of his lot. 'I labor pulling the plow from morning until night. No matter how hot is the day, or how tired my legs, or how the bow chafes my neck, I must still work. But you are a creature of leisure. You are trapped with a colorful blanket and do nothing more than carry our master about where he wishes to go. When he goes nowhere, you rest and eat green grass all day'.

"Now the ass, in spite of his vicious heels, was a goodly fellow and sympathized with the ox. 'My good friend', he replied, 'you do work very hard and I want to help ease your lot. Therefore, I will tell you how you can have a day of rest. In the morning when the slave comes to fetch you to the plow, lie on the ground and bellow so much that he says you are sick and cannot work'.

"So the ox took the advice of the ass and the next morning the slave returned to the farmer and told him the ox was sick and could not pull the plow.

"Then', said the farmer, 'hitch the ass to the plow for the plowing must go on'.

"All that day the ass, who had only intended to help his friend, found himself compelled to do the ox's task. When night came and he was released from the plow his heart was bitter and his legs were weary and his neck was sore where the bow had chafed it.

'The farmer lingered in the barnyard to listen.

'The ox began first. 'You are my good friend. Because of your wise advice I have enjoyed a day of rest'.

"And I," retorted the ass, 'am like many another simple hearted one who starts to help a friend and ends up by doing his task for him. Hereafter you draw your own plow, for I heard the master tell the slave to send for the butcher were you to be sick again. I wish he would, for you are a lazy fellow'. Thereafter they no longer spoke to each other and this ended their friendship. Can you tell me the moral to this tale, Rodan?"

"'It's a good tale," responded Rodan, "but I don't see the moral."

"I thought you wouldn't. But it is there and simple too. Just this: If you wish to help your friend, do so in a way that will not bring your friend's burdens upon yourself."

"I hadn't thought of that. It is a wise moral. I don't want to assume the burdens of my sister's husband. But tell me. You lend to many. Don't the borrowers repay?"

Mathon smiled the smile of one whose soul is rich with much experience. "Can a loan be well made if the borrower cannot repay? Musn't the lender be wise and judge carefully whether his gold can perform a useful purpose to the borrower and be returned to him once more; or whether it will be wasted by one unable to use it wisely and leave him without his treasure, and leave the borrower with a debt he cannot repay? I will show you the tokens in my token chest and let them tell you some of their stories."

He brought into the room a chest as long as his arm covered with red pigskin and ornamented with bronze designs. He placed it upon the floor and squatted before it, both hands upon the lid.

'From each person to whom I lend, I exact a token for my token chest, to remain there until the loan is repaid. When they repay I give it back, but if they never repay it will always remind me of one who was not faithful to my confidence.

'The safest loans, my token box tells me, are to those whose possessions are of more value than the loan they desire. They own lands or jewels, or camels, or other things which could be sold to repay the loan. Some of the tokens given to me are jewels of more value than the loan. Others are promises that if the loan is not repaid as agreed they will deliver to me certain property in settlement. On loans like those I am assured that my gold will be returned with the rental thereon, for the loan is based on property.

"In another class are those who have the capacity to earn. They are like you, who labor or serve and are paid. They have income and if they are honest and suffer no misfortune, I know that they can also repay the gold I loan them and the rental to which I am entitled. Such loans are based on human effort.

"Others are those who have neither property nor assured earning capacity. Life is hard and there will always be some who cannot adjust themselves to it. Alas for the loans I make them, even though they are not larger than a pence, my token box may censure me in the years to come unless they are guaranteed by good friends of the borrower who know him as honorable."

Mathon released the clasp and opened the lid. Rodan leaned forward eagerly.

At the top of the chest a bronze neckpiece lay upon a scarlet cloth. Mathon picked up the piece and patted it affectionately. "'This shall always remain in my token chest because the owner has passed on into the great darkness. I treasure it, his token, and I treasure his memory, for he was my good friend. We traded together with much success until he brought a woman out of the east to wed – beautiful, but not like our women. A dazzling creature. He spent his gold lavishly to gratify her desires. He came to me in distress when his gold was gone. I counseled with him. I told him I would help him to once more master his own affairs. He swore by the sign of the Great Bull that he would. But it was not to be. In a quarrel she thrust a knife into the heart he dared her to pierce."

"And she?" questioned Rodan.

"Yes, of course, this was hers." He picked up the scarlet cloth. "In bitter remorse she threw herself into the Euphrates. These two loans will never be repaid. The chest tells you, Rodan, that humans in the throws of great emotions are not safe risks for the gold lender.

"Here! Now this is different." He reached for a ring carved of ox bone. "This belongs to a farmer. I buy rugs from his women. The locusts came and they had not food. I helped him and when the new crop came he repaid me. Later he came again and told of strange goats in a distant land as described by a traveler. They had long hair so fine and soft it would weave into rugs more beautiful than any ever seen in Babylon. He wanted a herd but he had no money. So I lent him gold to make the journey and bring back goats. Now his herd is begun and next year I shall surprise the lords of Babylon with the most expensive rugs it has been their good fortune to buy. Soon I must return his ring. He insists on repaying promptly."

"Some borrowers do that?" queried Rodan.

"If they borrow for purposes that bring money back to them, I find it so. But if they borrow because of their indiscretions, I warn you to be cautious if you ever want to have your gold back in hand again."

'Tell me about this," requested Rodan, picking up a heavy gold bracelet inset with jewels in rare designs.

"The women appeal to my good friend," bantered Mathon.

"I am much younger than you," retorted Rodan.

"I grant that, but this time you suspect romance where there is none. The owner of this is fat and wrinkled, and talks so much and says so little she drives me mad. Once they had a lot of money and were my good customers, but ill times came upon them. She has a son who she wants to make a merchant. So she came to me and borrowed gold so that he might become a partner of a caravan owner who travels with his camels bartering in one city what he buys in another.

'This man proved to be a rascal for he left the poor boy in a distant city without money and without friends, pulling out early while the youth slept. Perhaps when this youth has grown to manhood, he will repay; until then I get no rental for the loan – only a lot of talk. But I do admit the jewels are worthy of the loan."

"Did this lady ask your advice as to the wisdom of the loan?"

"Quite otherwise. She had pictured to herself this son of hers as a wealthy and powerful man of Babylon. To suggest the contrary was to infuriate her. A fair rebuke I had. I knew the risk for this inexperienced boy, but since she offered security I couldn't refuse her.

'This," continued Mathon, waving a bit of pack rope tied into a knot, "belongs to Nebatur, the camel trader. When he buys a herd larger than his funds he brings this knot to me and I lend to him according to his needs. He is a wise trader. I have confidence in his good judgment and can lend him freely. Many other merchants of Babylon have my confidence because of their honorable behavior. Their tokens come and go frequently in my token box. Good merchants are an asset to our city and it profits me to aid them to keep trade moving so that Babylon can be prosperous."

Mathon picked out a beetle carved in turquoise and tossed it contemptuously. "A bug from Egypt. The lad who owns this does not care whether I ever receive back my gold; When I reproach him he replies, 'How can I repay when ill fate pursues me? You have plenty more'. What can I do, the token is his father's – a worthy man of small means who pledged his land and herd to back his son's enterprises. The youth found success at first and then was overzealous to gain great wealth. His knowledge was immature. His enterprises collapsed.

"Youth is ambitious. Youth take shortcuts to wealth and desirable things. To secure wealth quickly, youth often borrows unwisely. Youth, never having had experience, cannot realize that hopeless debt is like a deep pit into which one may descend quickly and where one may struggle vainly for many days. It is a pit of sorrow and regrets where the brightness of the sun is overcast and night is made unhappy by restless sleeping. Yet, I do not discourage borrowing gold. I encourage it. I recommend it if it's for a wise purpose. I myself made my first success as a merchant with borrowed gold.

"Yet, what should the lender do in such a situation? The youth is in despair and accomplishes nothing. He is discouraged. He makes no effort to repay. My heart turns against depriving the father of his land and cattle."

"You tell a lot that I am interested to hear," ventured Rodan, "but, I hear no answer to my question. Should I lend my fifty pieces of gold to my sister's husband? They mean a lot to me."

"Your sister is a sterling woman who I greatly esteem. If her husband came to me and asked to borrow fifty pieces of gold I would ask him for what purpose he would use it.

"If he answered that he desired to become a merchant like myself and deal in jewels and rich furnishings, I would say, 'What knowledge do you have of the ways of trade? Do you know where you can buy at the lowest cost? Do you know where you can sell at a fair price? Could he say 'Yes' to these questions?"

"No, he could not," Rodan admitted. "He has helped me in making spears and he has helped some in the shops."

'Then, would I say to him that his purpose was not wise. Merchants must learn their trade. His ambition, though worthy, is not practical and I would not lend him any gold. "But, supposing he could say, 'Yes, I have helped merchants a lot. I know how to travel to Smyrna and to buy rugs at a low cost. I also know many of the rich people of Babylon to whom I can sell these at a large profit.' Then I would say: 'Your purpose is wise and your ambition honorable. I shall be glad to lend you the fifty pieces of gold if you can give me security that they will be returned' But would he say, 'I have no security other than that I am an honored man and will pay you well for the loan.' Then would I reply, 'I treasure each piece of gold. If robbers took it from you as you journeyed to Smyrna or took the rugs from you as you returned, then you would have no means of repaying me and my gold would be gone!'

"Gold, you see, Rodan, is the merchandise of the lender of money. It is easy to lend. If it is lent unwisely then it is difficult to get back. The wise lender doesn't want the risk of the undertaking but the guarantee of safe repayment.

"'It is well," he continued, "to assist those that are in trouble, it is well to help those who fate has laid a heavy hand. It is well to help those who are starting so that they can progress and become valuable citizens. But help must be given wisely, lest, like the farmer's ass, in our desire to help we take upon ourselves the burden that belongs to another.

"Again I wandered from your question, Rodan, but hear my answer: Keep your fifty pieces of gold. What your labor earns for you and what is given to you as a reward is yours and no man can obligate you to part with it unless you want to. If you want to lend it so that it may earn you more gold, then lend it with caution and in many places. I don't like idle gold, and I like risk even less."

"How many years have you worked as a spear maker?"

"Three years."

"How much besides the King's gift have you saved?"

"Three gold pieces."

"Each year that you have labored, have you denied yourself good things in order to save from your earnings one piece of gold?"

"It is as you say."

'Then might you save in fifty years of labor fifty pieces of gold by your self-denial?"

"A lifetime of labor it would be."

"Do you think your sister would wish to jeopardize the savings of fifty years of labor over the hope that her husband might experiment on being a merchant?"

"Not if I spoke in your words."

"Then go to her and say, 'I have labored for three years, each day except fast days, from morning until night, and I have denied myself many things that my heart craved. For each year of labor and self-denial I have one piece of gold to show. You are my favorite sister and I want your husband to engage in business in which he will greatly prosper. If he can submit to me a plan that seems wise and possible to my friend, Mathon, then will I gladly lend to him my savings of an entire year so that he can have an opportunity to prove that he can succeed.' Do that, I say, and if he has the soul to succeed within him, he can prove it. If he fails, he will not owe you more than he can hope to some day repay.

"I am a gold lender because I own more gold than I can use in my own trade. I want my surplus gold to labor for others and thereby earn more gold. I don't want to risk losing my gold for I have labored greatly and denied myself greatly to secure it. Therefore, I will no longer lend any of it where I am not confident that it is safe and will be returned to me. Neither will I lend it where I am not convinced that its earnings will be promptly paid to me.

"I have told you, Rodan, a few of the secrets of my token chest. From them you can understand the weakness of men and their eagerness to borrow that which they have no certain means to repay. From this you can see how often their high hopes of the great earnings they could make – if they had gold – are but false hopes that they have not the ability or training to fulfill.

"You, Rodan, now have gold which you should put to earning more gold for you. You are about to become, as I, a gold lender. If you safely preserve your treasure it will produce great earnings for you and be a rich source of pleasure and profit your whole life. But if you let it escape from you, it will be a source of constant sorrow and regret for as long as you live.

"What do want most from the gold in your wallet?"

'To keep it safe."

"Wisely spoken," replied Mathon approvingly. 'Your first desire is for safety. Do you think that it would be truly safe from possible loss in the custody of your sister's husband?"

"I'm afraid not, for he is not wise in guarding gold."

"Then don't be swayed by foolish sentiments of obligation to trust your treasure to any person. If you want to help your family or friends, find other ways than risking the loss of your treasure. Don't forget that gold slips away in unexpected ways from those unskilled in guarding it. *You may as well waste your treasure in extravagances than let others lose it for you.*

"After safety, what else do you desire of your treasure?"

'That it earn more gold."

"Again you speak with wisdom. It should be made to earn and grow larger. Gold wisely lent may even double itself with its earnings before a man like you grows old. If you risk losing it you risk losing all that it would earn, as well.

"Therefore, don't be swayed by the fantastic plans of impractical men who think they see ways to force your gold to make unusually large earnings. *Such plans are the creations of dreamers unskilled in the safe and dependable laws of trade.* Be conservative in what you expect it to earn so that you can keep and enjoy your treasure. To hire it out with a promise of usurious returns is to invite loss.

"Seek to associate yourself with men and enterprises whose success is established so that your treasure can earn liberally under their skillful use and be guarded safely by their wisdom and experience.

"Thus, you can avoid the misfortunes that follow most of the sons of men to whom God entrusts gold."

When Rodan tried to thank him for his wise advice he would not listen, saying: "The king's gift will teach you wisdom. If you want to keep your fifty pieces of gold, you must be discreet indeed. Many uses will tempt you. Much advice will be given to you. Numerous opportunities to make large profits will be offered to you. The stories from my token box should warn you, before you let any piece of gold leave your pouch, to be sure that you have a safe way to pull it back again. Should my further advice appeal to you, return again. It is gladly given.

"Wherever you go, read that which I have carved beneath the lid of my token box. It applies equally to the borrower and the lender:

Better a Little Caution than a Great Regret".

THE TALE OF THE WALLS OF BABYLON

OLD BANZAR stood guard at the passageway leading to the top of the ancient walls of Babylon.

Up above, valiant defenders were battling to hold the walls. Upon them depended the future existence of this great city with its hundreds of thousands of citizens.

Over the walls came the roar of the attacking armies, the yelling of many men, the trampling of thousands of horses, the deafening boom of the battering rams pounding the bronzed gates.

In the street behind the gate lounged the spearmen, waiting to defend the entrance should the gates give way. They were but a few of the task. The main armies of Babylon were with their king, far away in the east on the great expedition against the Elamites. Since no attack upon the city was anticipated during their absence, the defending forces were small. Then unexpectedly, the mighty armies of the Assyrians bore down from the north. The walls must hold or Babylon was doomed.

About Banzar were great crowds of citizens, white faced and terrified, eagerly seeking news of the battle. With hushed awe they viewed the stream of wounded and dead being carried or led out of the passageway.

Here was the crucial point of attack. After three days of circling about the city, the enemy had suddenly thrown its great strength against this section and this gate.

The defenders from the top of the wall fought off the climbing platforms and the scaling ladders of the attackers with arrows, burning oil and lastly spears, if any reached the top. Thousands of the enemies' archers poured a deadly barrage of arrows against the defenders.

Old Banzar had the vantage point for news. He was closest to the conflict and first to hear of each fresh repulse of the frenzied attackers.

An elderly merchant crowded close to him, his palsied hands quivering. "Tell me! Tell me!" he pleaded. "They cannot get in. My sons are with the good king. There is no one to protect my old wife. My goods, they will steal everything. My food, they will leave nothing. We are old, too old to defend ourselves – too old for slaves. We will starve. We will die. Tell me they cannot get in."

"Calm yourself, good merchant," the guard responded. 'The walls of Babylon are strong. Go back to the bazaar and tell your wife that the walls will protect you and all of your possessions as safely as they protect the rich treasures of the king. Keep close to the walls, lest the arrows flying over, strike you!"

A woman with a babe in arms took the old man's place as he withdrew. "Sergeant, what news from the top? Tell me the truth so that I can reassure my poor husband. He lies with fever from his terrible wounds, yet insists upon his armor and his spear to protect me. He says the vengeful lust of our enemies will be terrible should they break in."

"Let your heart rest, good mother, the walls of Babylon will protect you and your babes. They are high and strong. Do you not hear the yells of our valiant defenders as they empty the caldrons of burning oil upon the ladder scalers?"

"Yes, I hear that, but I also hear the roar of the battering rams that hammer at our gates."

"Return to your husband. Tell him the gates are strong and can withstand the rams. Tell him the scalers climb the walls only to receive a thrust from the waiting spears. Watch your way and go quickly behind the buildings."

Banzar stepped aside to clear the passage for heavily armed reinforcements. As the clanking bronze shields and tread tramped by, a small girl plucked at his girdle.

"Tell me please, soldier, are we safe?" she pleaded. "I hear the awful noises. I see the men bleeding. I am so frightened. What will become of our family, of my mother, little brother and the baby?"

The grim old campaigner blinked his eyes and thrust forward his chin as he beheld the child.

"Be not afraid, little one," he reassured her. "The walls of Babylon will protect you and mother and little brother and the baby. It was for your safety that the good Queen Semiramis built them over a hundred years ago. Never have they been broken through. Go back and tell your mother and little brother and the baby that the walls of Babylon will protect them and they need have no fear."

Day after day old Banzar stood at his post and watched the reinforcements up the passageway, there to stay and fight until wounded or dead they came down once more. Around him, throngs of frightened citizens crowded unceasingly, seeking to learn if the walls would hold. To all he gave his answer with the fine dignity of an old soldier. "The walls of Babylon will protect you."

For three weeks and five days the attack waged with scarcely ceasing violence. Banzar's jaw became harder and grimmer as the passage behind, wet with the blood of the many wounded, was churned into mud by the never ceasing streams of men passing up and staggering down. Each day the slaughtered attackers piled up in heaps before the wall. Each night they were carried back and buried by their comrades.

On the fifth night of the fourth week the clamor diminished. The first streaks of daylight illuminating the plains disclosing great clouds of dust raised by the retreating armies.

A mighty shout went up from the defenders. There was no mistake in its meaning. It was repeated by the waiting troops behind the walls. It was echoed by the citizens in the street. It swept over the city with the violence of a storm.

People rushed from the houses. The streets were jammed with a throbbing mob. The pent-up fear of weeks found an outlet in the wild chorus of joy. From the top of the high tower of the Temple of Bel the flames of victory burst forth. The column of blue smoke floated skyward to carry the message far and wide.

The walls of Babylon had once again repulsed a mighty and vicious foe determined to loot her rich treasures and to ravish and enslave her citizens.

Babylon endured century after century because it was FULLY PROTECTED. It could not afford to be otherwise.

The walls of Babylon were an outstanding example of man's need and desire for protection. This desire is inherent in the human race. It is just as strong today as it ever was, but we have developed broader and better plans to accomplish the same purpose.

Today, behind the impregnable walls of insurance, savings accounts and dependable investments, we can guard ourselves against the unexpected tragedies that may enter any door and seat themselves before any fireside. We cannot afford to be without adequate protection.

THE TALE OF THE CAMEL TRADER OF BABYLON

THE hungrier one becomes the clearer one's mind works and the more sensitive one becomes to the odors of food.

For two days Tarkad, the son of Azure, had tasted no food except for two small figs purloined from over the wall of a garden before an angry Babylonian housekeeper chased him down the street. The woman's cries still rang in his ears and restrained his restless fingers from snatching tempting fruits from the baskets of the market women between whom he strolled.

He paced back and forth before the eating house hoping to meet someone he knew; someone from whom he could borrow a bit of copper that would gain him a friendly smile and a liberal helping from the fat keeper. Without the copper he knew how unwelcome he would be.

In his abstraction he unexpectedly found himself face to face with the tall bony figure of Dabasir, the camel trader.

"Ha! Here is Tarkad, who I have been looking for so that he will repay me the two pieces of copper I lent to him a month ago, and the piece of silver I lent him before that. It is good that we meet. I can use the coins this very day. What do you say, boy?"

Tarkad stuttered and his face flushed. He had little desire to encounter the outspoken Dabasir. "I am sorry, very sorry, but I don't have the copper nor the silver with which I could repay."

"Then get it! Surely you can get a few coppers and a piece of silver to repay the generosity of an old friend of your father who helped you when you were in need?"

"'It is because ill fortune pursues me that I cannot repay."

"Ill fortune! You blame God for your own weakness. Ill fortune pursues every man who thinks more of borrowing than of repaying. Come with me, boy, while I eat. I am hungry and I want to tell you a tale."

Tarkad flinched from the brutal frankness of Dabasir, but here at least was an invitation to enter the coveted doorway of the eating house.

Dabasir pushed him to a far corner of the room where they seated themselves upon small rugs.

When Kauskor, the proprietor, appeared smiling, Dabasir addressed him with his usual freedom. "Fat lizard of the desert, bring me a leg of goat very brown with much juice and bread and all of the vegetables for I am hungry and want food. Do not forget my friend here. Bring him a jug of water. Have it cooled, for the day is hot."

Tarkad's heart sank. Must he sit here and drink water while he watched this man devour an entire goat leg? He said nothing. He thought of nothing he could say.

Dabasir, however, knew no such thing as silence. Smiling and waving his hand good-naturedly to the other customers, all of whom knew him, he continued.

"I heard from a traveler who just returned from Urfa of a certain rich man who has a piece of stone cut so thin that one can look through it. He puts it in the window of his house to keep out the rains. It is yellow, this traveler tells, and he was permitted to look through it and the whole outside world looked strange and not like it really is. What do you say, Tarkad? Do you think the whole world could look a different color to a man than what it is?"

"I dare say," responded the youth, much more interested in the fat leg of goat placed before Dabasir.

"Well, I know I, myself, have seen the world all a different color from what it really is, and the tale I am about to tell relates how I came to see it in its right color once more."

"Dabasir will tell a tale," whispered a neighboring diner to his neighbor, and dragged his rug close. Other diners brought their food and crowded in a semi-circle. They crunched noisily Tarkad's ears and brushed him with their meaty bones. He alone was without food. Dabasir did not offer to share with him nor even motion him to a small corner of the hard bread that was broken off and had fallen from the platter to the floor.

"The tale that I am about to tell," began Dabasir, pausing to bite a goodly chunk from the goat leg, "relates to my early life and how I came to be a camel trader. Does anyone know that I once was a slave in Syria?"

A murmur of surprise ran through the audience to which Dabasir listened with satisfaction.

"When I was a young man," continued Dabasir after another vicious onslaught on the goat leg, "I learned my father's trade, the making of saddles. I worked with him in his shop and got married. Being young and not greatly skilled, I could earn but little, just enough to support my excellent wife in a modest way. I craved good things which I could not afford. Soon I found that the shopkeepers would trust me to pay later even though I could not pay at the time. So I indulged my desires and wore fine attire and bought many things for my wife and my home beyond the reach of my earnings. I paid as I could and for a while, all went well. But in time I discovered I could not use my earnings both to live upon and to pay my debts. Creditors began to pursue me to pay for my extravagant purchases and my life became miserable. I borrowed from my friends, but could not repay them either. Things went from bad to worse. My wife returned to her father and I decided to leave Babylon and seek another city where as I thought a young man might have a chance to succeed.

"For two years I led a restless and unsuccessful life working for caravan traders. From this I fell in with a set of likeable robbers who scoured the desert for unarmed caravans. Such deeds were unworthy of the son of my father, but I was seeing the world through a colored stone and did not realize to what degradation I had fallen.

"We met with success on our first trip, capturing a rich haul of gold and silks and valuable merchandise. We took this loot to Ginir and squandered. The second time we were not so fortunate. Just after we had made our capture, we were attacked by the spearsmen of a native chief whom the caravans paid for protection. Our two leaders were killed and the rest of us were taken to Damascus where we were stripped of our clothing and sold as slaves.

"I was purchased for two pieces of silver by a Syrian desert chief. With my hair shorn and only a loin cloth to wear, I was not so different from the other slaves. Being a reckless youth, I thought it merely an adventure until my master took me before his four wives and told them they could have me for a eunuch.

"Then, indeed, I realized the hopelessness of my situation. These men of the desert were fierce and warlike. I was subject to their will without weapons or means of escape.

"I stood fearful, as those four women looked me over. I wondered if I could expect pity from them. Sira, the first wife, was older than the others. Her face was impassive as she looked upon me. I turned from her with little consolation. The next was a contemptuous beauty who gazed at me as indifferently as if I had been a worm of the earth. The two younger ones tittered as though it were all an exciting joke.

It seemed an age that I stood waiting sentence. Each woman appeared willing for the others to decide. Finally Sira spoke up in a cold voice.

"Of eunuchs we have plenty, but of camel tenders we have few and they are a worthless lot. Today I want to visit my mother who is sick with fever and there is no slave I would trust to lead my camel. Ask this slave if he can lead a camel."

"My master thereupon questioned me. 'What do you know of camels?'

"Striving to conceal my eagerness, I replied, 'I can make them kneel, I can load them, I can lead them on long trips without tiring. If need be, I can repair their trappings.'

"'The slave speaks forward enough,' observed my master. 'If you want, Sira, take this man as your camel tender.'

"So I was turned over to Sira and that day I led her camel upon a long journey to her sick mother. I took the occasion to thank her for her intercession and also to tell her that I was not a slave by birth, but the son of a freeman, an honorable saddle maker of Babylon. I also told her much of my story. Her comments were disconcerting to me and I pondered greatly afterwards on what she said.

"How can you call yourself a free man when your weakness has brought you to this? If a man has in himself the soul of a slave will he not become one no matter what his birth, even as water seeks its level? If a man has within him the soul of a free man, will he not become respected and honored in his own city in spite of his misfortune?'

"For over a year I was a slave and lived with the slaves, but I could not become as one of them. One day Sira asked me, 'In the evening time, when the other slaves mingle and enjoy each other's company, do you tent alone?'

"To which I responded, 'I am thinking of what you said to me. I wonder if I have the soul of a slave. I cannot join them, so I sit apart.'

'I, too, must sit apart', she confided. 'My dowry was large and my lord married me because of it. Yet he does not want me. What every woman longs for is to be desired. Because of this and because I am barren and have neither son nor daughter, I must sit apart. If I were a man, I would rather die than be such a slave, but the conventions of our tribe make slaves of women.'

"Have I the soul of a man or have I the soul of a slave? What do you think?' I asked.

"*Do you have a desire to repay the debts you owe in Babylon?'*

"Yes, I have the desire, but I see no way.'

"'If you contentedly let the years slip by and make no effort to repay, then you have the contemptible soul of a slave. No man is otherwise who cannot respect himself and *no man can respect himself who does not repay honest debts.'*

"But what can I do, as I am slave in Syria?"

"Stay a slave in Syria, you weakling.'

"I am not a weakling', I denied hotly.

"Then prove it.'

"How?"

"Does your great king not fight his enemies in every way he can and with every force he has? Your debts are your enemies that have run you out of Babylon. You left them alone and they grew too strong for you. Had you fought them as a man, you could have conquered them and been honored among your townspeople. But you didn't have the soul to fight them and behold you have gone down until you are a slave in Syria.'

"I thought a lot about her unkind accusations and worded many defenses I could use to prove myself not a slave at heart, but I was not to have the chance to use them. Three days later Sira's maid took me to her mistress.

'My mother is again very sick', she said. 'Saddle the two best camels in my husband's herd. Tie on water skins and saddlebags for a long journey. The maid will give you food at the kitchen tent.' I packed the camels, wondering about the quantity of provisions the maid provided, for the mother lived less than a day's journey away. The maid rode the rear camel and I led the camel of my mistress. When we reached her mother's house it was just dark. Sira dismissed the maid and said to me:

"Do you have the soul of a free man or the soul of a slave?'

"The soul of a free man', I responded.

"Now is your chance to prove it. Your master has drunk heavily and he and his chiefs are in a stupor. Take these camels and make your escape. Here in this bag are clothes belonging to your master to disguise you. I will say you stole the camels and ran away while I visited my sick mother."

"You have the soul of a queen," I told her. 'I wish I could lead you to happiness.'

"'Happiness', she responded, 'does not await a runaway wife who seeks it in far lands among strange people. Go on your way and may God of the desert protect you, for the way is far and devoid of food or water.'

"I needed no further urging, but thanked her warmly and was away into the night. I didn't know this strange country and had only a dim idea of the direction in which Babylon lay, but struck out bravely across the desert toward the hills. One camel I rode and the other I led. All that night and the next day I traveled, urged on by the knowledge of the terrible fate that was meted out to slaves who stole their master's property and tried to escape.

"Late that afternoon, I reached a rough country as uninhabitable as the desert. The sharp rocks bruised the feet of my faithful camels and soon they were picking their way slowly and painfully along. I met neither man nor beast and could well understand why they shunned this inhospitable land.

"It was a journey that few men live to tell of. Day after day we plodded along. Food and water gave out. The heat of the sun was merciless. At the end of the ninth day, I slid from the back of my mount with the feeling that I was too weak to ever remount and that I would surely die, lost in this abandoned country.

"I stretched out on the ground and slept, not waking until the first gleam of daylight.

"I sat up and looked about me. There was a coolness in the morning air. My camels lay dejected not far away. About me was a vast waste of broken country covered with rock and sand and thorny things, no sign of water, nothing to eat for man or camel.

"Could it be that in this peaceful quiet I faced my end? My mind was clearer than it had ever been before. My body now seemed of little importance. My parched and bleeding lips, my dry and swollen tongue, my empty stomach, all had lost their supreme importance of the day before.

"I looked across into the uninviting distance and once again the question came to me, 'Have I the soul of a slave or the soul of a free man?' *Then with clearness I realized that if I had the soul of a slave, I would give up, lie down in the desert and die, a fitting end for a runaway slave.*

"But if I had the soul of a free man, what then? Surely I would force my way back to Babylon, repay the people who had trusted me, bring happiness to my wife who had cared for me, bring peace and contentment to my parents.

"Your debts are your enemies who have run you out of Babylon', Sira had said. Yes, it was so. Why had I refused to stand my ground like a man? Why had I permitted my wife to go back to her father? Why had I been weak like a slave if I had not the soul of one?

'Then a strange thing happened. The whole world seemed to be of a different color as though I had been looking at it through a colored stone that had suddenly been removed. At last I saw the true values in life.

"Die in the desert! Not I! With a new vision, I saw the things that I must do. First I would go back to Babylon and face every man who I owed an unpaid debt. I would tell them that after years of wandering and misfortune, I had come back to pay my debts as fast as God would permit. Next I would make a home for my wife and become a citizen of whom my parents would be proud.

"My debts were my enemies, but the men I owed were my friends for they had trusted me and believed in me.

"I staggered weakly to my feet. What did hunger matter? What did thirst matter? They were but incidents on the road to Babylon. *Within me surged the soul of a free man going back to conquer his enemies and reward his friends.* I thrilled with the great resolve.

"The glazed eyes of my camels brightened at the new note in my husky voice. With great effort, after many attempts, they gained their feet. With pitiful perseverance, they pushed on toward the north where something within me said we would find Babylon.

"We found water. We passed into a more fertile country where there was grass and fruit. We found the trail to Babylon because the soul of a free man looks at life as a series of problems to be solved and solves them, while the soul of a slave whines, 'What can I do since I am a slave?'

"How about you, Tarkad? Does your empty stomach make your head exceedingly clear? Are you ready to take the road that leads to Babylon?"

97

Moisture came to the eyes of the youth. He rose eagerly to his knees. 'You have shown me a vision; already I feel the soul of a free man surge within me."

Again Dabasir turned to his food. "Kauskor, you snail", he called loudly to be heard in the kitchen, "the food is cold. Bring me more meat fresh from the roasting. Bring also a portion for Tarkad the son of my old friend who is hungry and who will eat with me."

So ended the tale of Dabasir the camel trader of old Babylon. He found his soul when he realized a great truth, a truth that had been known and used by wise men long before his time.

It has led men of all ages out of difficulties and into success, and it will continue to do so for those who have the wisdom to understand its magic power. *It is for any man to use who reads these lines.*

Where there is Determination, the Way Can Be Found

THE TALE OF THE CLAY TABLETS FROM BABYLON

ST. SWITHIN'S COLLEGE
NOTTINGHAM UNIVERSITY
NEWARK-ON-TRENT
NOTTINGHAM

October 21,1934.

Professor Franklin Caldwell,
Care of British Scientific Expedition,
Hillah, Mesopotamia.

My dear Professor:

The five clay tablets from your recent excavation in the ruins of Babylon arrived on the same boat with your letter. I have been fascinated to no end, and have spent many pleasant hours translating their inscriptions. I would have answered your letter at once but delayed until I could complete the translations which are attached.

The tablets arrived without damage, thanks to your careful use of preservatives and excellent packing.

You will be as astonished as we were in the laboratory, about the story they relate. One expects the dim and distant past to speak of romance and adventure. "Arabian Nights" sort of thing, you know.

When instead it discloses the problem of a person named Dabasir, to pay off his debts, one realizes that conditions upon this old world have not changed as much in five thousand years as one might expect.

It's odd, you know, but these old inscriptions rather 'rag' me, as the students say. Being a college professor, I am supposed to be a thinking human being possessed with a working knowledge upon most subjects. Yet, here comes this old chap out of the dust-covered ruins of Babylon to offer a way I had never heard of, to pay off my debts and at the same time acquire gold to jingle in my wallet.

Pleasant thought, I say, and interesting to prove whether it will work as well nowadays as it did in old Babylon. Mrs. Shrewsbury and myself are planning to try his plan out on our own affairs which could be much improved.

Wishing you the best of luck in your worthy undertaking and waiting eagerly another opportunity to assist, I am,

Yours sincerely,
Alfred H. Shrewsbury,
Department of Archaeology.

TABLET No. 1

When the moon becomes full, I, Dabasir, who but recently returned from slavery in Syria, with the determination to pay my many debts and become a man of means worthy of respect in my native city of Babylon, do here engrave upon the clay a permanent record of my affairs to guide and assist me in carrying through my wishes.

Under the wise advice of my good friend Mathon, the gold lender, I am determined to follow an exact plan that he says will lead any honorable man out of debt into means and self-respect.

This plan includes three purposes that are my hope and desire.

First, the PLAN provides for my future prosperity.

Therefore one-tenth of all I earn shall be set aside as my own to keep. For Mathon speaks wisely when he says:

"The man who keeps both gold and silver in his purse that he does not spend is good to his family and loyal to his king.

"The man who has but a few coppers in his purse, is indifferent to his family and indifferent to his king.

"But the man who has nothing in his purse is unkind to his family and is disloyal to his king for his heart is bitter.

"Therefore, the man who wishes to achieve must have coins he can jingle in his purse, so that he can have love in his heart for his family and loyalty to his king."

Second, the PLAN provides that I will support and clothe my good wife who has returned to me with loyalty from her father's house. For Mathon says that to take good care of a faithful wife puts self-respect into the heart of a man and adds strength and determination to his purposes.

Therefore seven-tenths of all I earn will be used to provide a home, clothes to wear, and food to eat, with a bit extra to spend so that our lives are not lacking in pleasure and enjoyment. But Mathon further cautions the greatest care that we spend no more than seven-tenths of what I earn for these worthy purposes. Herein lies the success of the PLAN. I must live upon this portion and never use more, nor buy what I cannot pay for, out of this portion.

TABLET No. II

Third, the PLAN provides that my debts will be paid out of my earnings.

Therefore each month, two-tenths of all I have earned will be divided honorably and fairly among those who have trusted me and to whom I am indebted. Thus in due time all my indebtedness will surely be paid.

Therefore, I engrave here the names of every man to whom I am indebted and the honest amount of my debt.

Fahru, the cloth weaver, 2 silver, 6 copper.

Sinjar, the couch maker, 1 silver.

Ahrnar, my friend, 3 silver, 1 copper.

Zankar, my friend, 4 silver, 7 copper.

Askanir, my friend, 1 silver, 3 copper.

Harinsir, the jewel maker, 6 silver, 2 copper.

Diarbeker, my father's friend, 4 silver, 1 copper.

Alkahad, the house owner, 14 silver.

Mathon, the gold lender, 9 silver.

Birejik, the farmer, 1 silver, 7 copper.

(From here on, disintegrated. Cannot be deciphered.)

TABLET No. III

To these creditors I owe in total one hundred and nineteen pieces of silver and one hundred and forty-one pieces of copper. Because I owed these sums and saw no way to repay, in my folly I permitted my wife to return to her father and left my native city and sought easy wealth elsewhere, only to find disaster and to see myself sold into the degradation of slavery.

Now that Mathon has shown me how I can repay my debts in small sums out of my earnings, I realize the great extent of my folly in running away from the results of my extravagances.

Therefore have I visited my creditors and explained to them that I have no resources with which to pay except my ability to earn, and that I intend to apply two-tenths of all I earn upon my indebtedness, evenly and honestly. This much can I pay but no more. Therefore if they are patient, in time my obligations will be paid in full.

Ahmar, who I thought was my best friend, reviled me bitterly and I left him in humiliation. Birejik, the farmer, pleaded that I pay him first as he badly needed help. Alkahad, the house-owner, was indeed disagreeable and insisted that he would make trouble for me unless I soon settled in full with him.

All the rest willingly accepted my proposal. Therefore am I more determined than ever to carry through, being convinced that it is easier to pay one's just debts than to avoid them. Even though I cannot meet the needs and demands of a few of my creditors, I will deal impartially with all.

TABLET No. IV

Again the moon shines full. I have worked hard with a free mind. My good wife has supported my intentions to pay my creditors. Because of our wise determination, I have earned during the past month – buying camels of sound wind and good legs for Nebatur – the sum of nineteen pieces of silver.

This I have divided according to the PLAN. One-tenth I have set aside to keep as my own, seven-tenths I have divided with my good wife to pay for our living. Two-tenths I have divided among my creditors as evenly as could be done in coppers.

I did not see Ahmar, but left it with his wife. Birejik was so pleased he would kiss my hand. Only old Alkahad was grouchy and said I must pay faster. To which I replied that if I were permitted to be well fed and not worried, that alone would enable me to pay faster. All the others thanked me and spoke well of my efforts.

Therefore, at the end of one month, my indebtedness is reduced by almost four pieces of silver and I possess almost two pieces of silver besides, upon which no man has claim. My heart is lighter than it has been for a long time.

Again the moon shines full. I have worked hard but with poor success. I have been able to buy few camels. I have earned only eleven pieces of silver. Nevertheless, my good wife and I have stood by the plan even though we have bought no new clothing and eaten little but herbs. Again I paid ourselves one-tenth of the eleven pieces, while we lived upon seven-tenths. I was surprised when Ahmar commended my payment, even though small. So did Birejik. Alkahad flew into a rage but when told to give back his portion if he did not want it, he calmed down. The others were content as before.

Again the moon shines full and I am greatly rejoiced. I intercepted a fine herd of camels and bought many sound ones, therefore my earnings were forty-two pieces of silver. This month my wife and myself have bought much-needed sandals and clothing. We have also dined well on meat and fowl.

We have paid more than eight pieces of silver to our creditors. Even Alkahad did not protest.

Great is the PLAN for it leads us out of debt and gives us wealth which is ours to keep.

Three times the moon has been full since I last carved upon this clay. Each time I paid myself one-tenth of all I earned. Each time my good wife and I have lived upon seven-tenths even though at times it was difficult. Each time have I paid my creditors two-tenths. In my purse I now have twenty-one pieces of silver that are mine. It makes my head stand straight upon my shoulders and makes me proud to walk among my friends.

My wife keeps our home well and is becomingly dressed. We are happy to live together.

The PLAN is of untold value. Has it not made an honorable man of an ex-slave?

TABLET No. V

Again the moon shines full and I remember that it has been a long time since I carved upon the clay. In truth, twelve months have come and gone. But today I will not neglect my record because today I have paid the last of my debts. This is the day upon which my good wife and my thankful self celebrate with great feasting that our goal has been accomplished.

Many things occurred upon my final visit to my creditors that I will long remember. Ahmar begged my forgiveness for his unkind words and said that I was the one out of all the others he most desired for a friend.

Old Alkahad is not so bad after all, for he said. "You were once a piece of soft clay to be pressed and molded by any hand that touched you, but now you are a piece of bronze capable of holding an edge. If you need silver or gold at any time come to me."

Nor is he the only man who holds me in high regard. Many others speak deferentially to me. My good wife looks upon me with a light in her eyes that makes a man have confidence in himself.

Yet it is the PLAN that has made me successful. It has enabled me to pay all my debts and to jingle both gold and silver in my purse. I recommend it to all who wish to get ahead. For if it will enable an ex-slave to pay his debts and have gold in his purse, will it not aid any man to find independence? Nor am I, myself, finished with it, for I am convinced that if I follow it further it will make me rich among men.

ST. SWITHIN'S COLLEGE
NOTTINGHAM UNIVERSITY
NEWARK-ON-TRENT
NOTTINGHAM

November 7th, 1936

Professor Franklin Caldwell,
Care of British Scientific Expedition,
Hillah, Mesopotamia

My dear professor:

If, in your further digging into those bally ruins of Babylon, you encounter the ghost of a former resident, an old camel trader named Dabasir, do me a favor. Tell him that his scribbling upon those clay tablets, so long ago, has earned for him the life-long gratitude of couple of college folks back here in England.

You will possibly remember my writing a year ago that Mrs. Shrewsbury and myself intended to try his plan for getting out of debt and at the same time having gold to jingle. You may have guessed, even though we tried to keep it from our friends, our desperate straits.

We were frightfully humiliated for years by a lot of old debts and were worried sick for fear that some of the trades people might start a scandal that would force me out of the college. We paid and paid every shilling we could squeeze out of my income, but it was hardly enough to hold things even. Besides we were forced to do all our buying where we could get further credit regardless of higher costs.

It developed into one of those vicious circles that grow worse instead of better. Our struggles were getting hopeless. We could not move to less costly rooms because we owed the landlord. There did not appear to be anything we could do to improve our situation.

Then, here comes your acquaintance, the old camel trader from Babylon, with a plan to do just what we wished to accomplish. He jolly well stirred us up to follow his system. We made a list of all our debts and I took it around and showed it to every one we owed.

I explained how it was simply impossible for me to ever pay them the way things were going along. They could readily see this themselves from the figures. Then I explained that the only way I saw to pay in full was to set aside twenty percent of my income each month to be divided pro rata, which would pay them in full in a little over two years; that, in the meantime, we would go on a cash basis and give them the further benefit of our cash purchases.

They were really quite decent. Our green grocer, a wise old chap, put it in a way that helped to bring around the rest. "If you pay for all you buy and then pay some on what you owe, that is better than you have done, for ye ain't paid down the account none in three years."

Finally I secured all their names to an agreement binding them not to molest us as long as
the twenty percent of income was paid regularly. Then we began scheming on how to live upon seventy per cent. We were determined to keep that extra ten per cent to jingle. The thought of silver and possibly gold was most alluring.

It was like having an adventure to make the change. We enjoyed figuring this way and that to live comfortably upon that remaining seventy per cent. Started with rent and managed to secure a fair reduction. Next we put our favorite brands of tea and such under suspicion and were agreeably surprised how often we could purchase superior qualities at less cost.

It is too long a story for a letter but anyhow it did not prove difficult. We managed and right cheerfully at that. What a relief it proved to have our affairs in such a shape we were no longer persecuted by past due accounts.

I must not neglect, however, to tell you about that extra ten percent we were supposed to jingle. Well, we did jingle it for some time. Now don't laugh too soon. You see, that is the sporty part. It is the real fun, to start accumulating money that you do not want to spend. There is more pleasure in running up such a surplus than there could be in spending it.

After we had jingled to our hearts content, we found a more profitable use for it. We took on an investment into which we could pay that ten per cent each month. This is proving to be the most satisfying part of our regeneration. It is the first thing we pay out of my check.

There is a most gratifying sense of security to know our investment is growing steadily. By the time my teaching days are over it should be a snug sum, large enough so the income will take care of us from then on.

All this out of my same old check. Difficult to believe, yet absolutely true. All our old debts are gradually being paid and at the same time our investment is increasing. Besides, we get along financially even better than before. Who would believe there could be such a difference in results between following a financial plan and just drifting along?

At the end of the next year, when all our old bills will have been paid, we will have more to pay into our investment besides some extra for travel. We are determined never again to permit our living expenses to exceed seventy percent of our income.

Now you can understand why we would like to extend our personal thanks to that old chap whose plan saved us from our 'Hell on Earth', DEBTS.

He knew. He had been through it all He wanted others to benefit from his own bitter experiences. That is why he spent tedious hours carving his message upon the clay.

He had a real message for fellow sufferers, a message so important that after five thousand years it has risen out of the ruins of Babylon, just as true and just as vital as the day it was buried.

Yours sincerely,
Alfred H. Shrewsbury,
Department of Archaeology.

HISTORICAL SKETCH OF BABYLON

In the pages of history, there lives no city more glamorous than Babylon. Its very name conjures visions of wealth and splendor. Its treasures of gold and jewels were fabulous. One naturally pictures such a wealthy city as located in a suitable setting of tropical luxuriance, surrounded by rich natural resources of forests and mines. Such was not the case. It was located beside the Euphrates River, in a flat, arid valley. It had no forests, no mine, not even stone for building. It was not even located upon a natural trade route. The rainfall was insufficient to raise crops.

Babylon is an outstanding example of man's ability to achieve great objectives using whatever means are at his disposal. All of the resources supporting this large city were man developed. All of its riches were man made.

Babylon possessed just two natural resources – a fertile soil and water in the river. With one of the greatest engineering accomplishments of this or any other day, Babylonian engineers diverted the waters from the river by means of dams and immense irrigation canals. Far out across that arid valley went these canals to pour the life-giving waters over the fertile soil. This ranks among the first engineering feats known to history. Such abundant crops as were the reward of this irrigation system here, we doubt if the world had ever seen before.

Fortunately, during its long existence, Babylon was ruled by successive lines of kings to whom conquest and plunder were but incidental. While it engaged in many wars, most of these were local or defensive against ambitious conquerors from other countries who coveted the fabulous "Treasures of Babylon". The outstanding rulers of Babylon live on in history because of their wisdom, enterprise and justice. Babylon produced no strutting monarchs who sought to conquer the known world so that all nations might pay homage to their egotism.

As a city, Babylon exists no more. When those energizing human forces that built and maintained the city for thousands of years were withdrawn, it soon became a deserted ruin. The site of the city is in Asia about six hundred miles east of the Suez Canal, just north of the Persian Gulf. The latitude is about 30 degrees above the Equator, practically the same as that of Yuma, Arizona. It possessed a climate similar to that of this American city, hot and dry.

Today, this valley of the Euphrates, once a populous irrigated farming district, is again the wind swept arid waste. Scant grass and desert shrubs strive for existence against the wind blown sands. Gone are the fertile fields, the mammoth cities and the long caravans of rich merchandise. Nomadic bands of Arabs, securing a scant living by tending small herds are the only inhabitants. Such it has been since about the beginning of the Christian era.

Dotting this valley are earthen hills. For centuries, they were considered by travelers to be nothing else. The attention of archaeologists was finally attracted to them because of pieces of pottery and brick washed down by the occasional rainstorms. Expeditions, financed by European and American Museums, were sent here to excavate and see what could be found. Picks and shovels soon proved these hills to be ancient cities. City graves, they might well be called.

Babylon was one of these. Over it for something like twenty centuries, the winds had scattered the desert dust. Built originally of brick, all exposed walls had disintegrated and gone back to earth once more. Such is Babylon, the wealthy city, today. A heap of dirt, so long abandoned that no living person even knew its name until it was discovered by carefully removing the refuse of centuries from the streets and the fallen wreckage of its noble temples and palaces.

Many scientists consider the civilization of Babylon and other cities in this valley to be the oldest of which there is a definite record. Positive dates have been proved reaching back 8000 years. An interesting fact in this connection is the means used to

112

determine these dates. Uncovered in the ruins of Babylon, were descriptions of an eclipse of the sun. Modern astronomers readily computed the time when such an eclipse, visible in Babylon, occurred and thus established a known relationship between their calendar and our own.

In this way, we have proved that 8000 years ago the Sumerites, who inhabited Babylonia, were living in walled cities. One can only conjecture for how many centuries previous such cities had existed. Their inhabitants were not mere barbarians living within protecting walls. They were an educated and enlightened people. So far as written history goes, they were the first engineers, the first astronomers, the first mathematicians, the first financiers and the first people to have a written language.

Mention has already been made of the irrigation systems that transformed the arid valley into an agricultural paradise. The remains of these canals can still be traced, although they are mostly filled with accumulated sand. Some of them were of such size that, when empty of water, a dozen horses could be ridden along their bottoms abreast. In size they compare favorably with the largest canals in Colorado and Utah.

In addition to irrigating the valley lands, Babylonian engineers completed another project of similar magnitude. By means of an elaborate drainage system they reclaimed an immense area of swamp land at the mouths of the Euphrates and Tigris Rivers and put this also under cultivation.

Herodotus, the Greek traveler and historian, visited Babylon while it was in its prime and has given us the only known description by an outsider. His writings give a graphic description of the city and some of the unusual customs of its people. He mentions the remarkable fertility of the soil and the bountiful harvests of wheat and barley which they produced.

The glory of Babylon has faded but its wisdom has been preserved for us. For this we are indebted to their form of records. In that distant day, the use of paper had not been invented. Instead, they laboriously engraved their writing upon tablets of moist clay. When completed, these were baked and became hard tile. In size, they were about six by eight inches and an inch in thickness.

These day tablets, as they are commonly called, were used much as we use modem forms of writing. Upon them were engraved lengthy legends, rare poetry, history, transcriptions of royal decrees, the laws of the lands, titles to property, promissory notes and even letters which were dispatched by messengers to distant cities. From these day tablets we are permitted an insight into the intimate personal affairs of the people. For example, one tablet, evidently from the records of a country storekeeper, relates that upon the given date a certain named customer brought in a cow and exchanged it for seven sacks of wheat, three being delivered at the time and the other four to await the customer's pleasure.

Another gives a part of the autobiography of Ashurbanipal, one of their kings. Among other things, he advises us: "The beautiful writing in Sumerian, that is difficult to remember, it was my joy to repeat. I directed the weaving of reed shields and breastworks like a pioneer. I had the learning that all clerks of every kind possess when their time of maturity comes. At the same time I learned what is proper for lordship."

Safely buried in the wrecked cities, archaeologists have recovered entire libraries of these
tablets, hundreds of thousands of them.

Of the outstanding wonders of Babylon were the immense walls surrounding the city. The ancients ranked them with the great pyramid of Egypt, as belonging to the "Seven Wonders of the world". Queen Semiramis is credited with having erected the first walls during the early history of the city. Modern excavators have been unable to find any trace of the original walls. Nor is their exact height known. From mention made by early writers, it is estimated they were about fifty to sixty feet high, faced on the outer side with burned brick and further protected by a deep moat of water.

The later and more famous walls were started about six hundred years before the time of Christ by King Nabopolassar. Upon such a gigantic scale did he plan the rebuilding, he did not live to see the work finished. This was left to his son, Nebuchadnezzar, whose name is familiar in Biblical history.

The height and length of these later walls staggers belief. They are reported upon reliable authority to have been about one hundred and sixty feet high, the equivalent of the height of a modern fifteen-story office building. The total length is estimated as between nine and eleven miles. So wide was the top, that a six-horse chariot could be driven around them. Of this tremendous structure, little now remains except portions of the foundations and the moat. In addition to the ravages of the elements, the Arabs completed the destruction by quarrying the brick for building purposes elsewhere.

Against the walls of Babylon marched, in turn, the victorious armies of almost every victorious conqueror of that age of wars of conquest. A host of kings laid siege to Babylon, but always in vain. Invading armies of that day were not to be considered lightly. Historians speak of such units as 10,000 horsemen, 25,000 chariots, 1200 regiments of foot soldiers with 1000 men to the regiment. Often two to three years of preparation would be required to assemble war materials and depots of food along the proposed line of march.

The city of Babylon was organized much like a modem city. There were streets and shops. Peddlers offered their wares through residential districts. Priests officiated in magnificent temples. Within the city was an inner enclosure for the royal palaces. The walls about this were said to have been higher than those about the city.

The Babylonians were skilled in the arts. These included sculpture, painting, weaving, gold working and the manufacture of metal weapons and agricultural implements. Their jewelers created most artistic jewelry. Many samples have been recovered from the graves of its wealthy citizens and are now on exhibition in the leading museums of the world.

At a very early period when the rest of world was still hacking at trees with stone headed axes, or hunting and fighting with flint pointed spears and arrows, the Babylonians were using axes, spears and arrows with metal heads.

The Babylonians were clever financiers and traders. So far as we know, they were the original inventors of money as a means of exchange, of promissory notes and written titles to property.

Babylon was never entered by hostile armies until about 540 years before the birth of Christ. Even then the walls were not captured. The story of the fall of Babylon is most unusual. Cyrus, one of the great conquerors of that period, intended to attack the city and hoped to take its impregnable walls. Advisors of Nabonidus, the King of Babylon, persuaded him to go forth to meet Cyrus and give him battle without waiting for the city to be besieged.

In the succeeding battle Cyrus administered such an astounding defeat to the Babylonian army, it fled away from the city. Cyrus, thereupon, entered the open gates and took possession without resistance.

Thereafter the power and prestige of the city gradually waned until, in the course of a few hundred years, it was eventually abandoned, deserted, left for the winds and storm to level once again to that desert earth from which its grandeur had originally been built. Babylon had fallen, never to rise again, but to it civilization owes much.

The eons of time have crumbled to dust the proud walls of its temples, but the wisdom of Babylon endures.

116

BN Publishing

Improving People's Life

www.bnpublishing.com

We Have Book Recommendations for You

The Strangest Secret by Earl Nightingale (Audio CD - Jan 2006)

Acres of Diamonds [MP3 AUDIO] [UNABRIDGED] (Audio CD) by Russell H. Conwell

Automatic Wealth: The Secrets of the Millionaire Mind - Including: Acres of Diamonds, As a Man Thinketh, I Dare you!, The Science of Getting Rich, The Way to Wealth, and Think and Grow Rich [UNABRIDGED] by Napoleon Hill, et al (CD-ROM)

Think and Grow Rich [MP3 AUDIO] [UNABRIDGED] by Napoleon Hill, Jason McCoy (Narrator) (Audio CD - January 30, 2006)

As a Man Thinketh [UNABRIDGED] by James Allen, Jason McCoy (Narrator) (Audio CD)

Your Invisible Power: How to Attain Your Desires by Letting Your Subconscious Mind Work for You [MP3 AUDIO] [UNABRIDGED]

Thought Vibration or the Law of Attraction in the Thought
World [MP3 AUDIO] [UNABRIDGED]
by William Walker Atkinson, Jason McCoy (Narrator) (Audio
CD - July 1, 2005)

The Law of Success Volume I: The Principles of Self-Mastery
by Napoleon Hill (Audio CD - Feb 21, 2006)

The Law of Success, Volume I: The Principles of Self-Mastery
(Law of Success, Vol. 1) (The Law of Success) by Napoleon Hill
(Paperback - Jun 20, 2006)

The Law of Success, Volumes II & III: A Definite Chief Aim &
Self -Confidence by Napoleon Hill (Paperback - Jun 20, 2006)

Thought Vibration or the Law of Attraction in the Thought
World & Your Invisible Power (Paperback)

BN Publishing

Improving People's Life

www.bnpublishing.com

Printed in the United States
205066BV00003B/49-60/A

9 789562 914109